T0198705

Gifted Education and GIFTED STUDENTS

Gifted Education *and* GIFTED STUDENTS

A Guide for Inservice and Preservice Teachers

Kelly C. Margot, Ph.D.,
and Jacque Melin

NEW YORK AND LONDON

First published in 2020 by Prufrock Press Inc.

Published in 2021 by Routledge
605 Third Avenue, New York, NY 10017
2 Park Square, Milton Park, Abingdon, Oxon OX14 4RN

Routledge is an imprint of the Taylor & Francis Group, an informa business.

Cover design by Allegra Denbo and layout design by Raquel Trevino

Library of Congress Control Number:2019952488

ISBN-13: 978-1-6182-1893-3 (pbk)

DOI: 10.4324/9781003235330

TABLE OF CONTENTS

INTRODUCTION
Intentionally Teaching Gifted Learners 1

CHAPTER 1
Gifted Learners: Research, Theories, and Models 5

CHAPTER 2
Underrepresented Populations in Gifted Education 15

CHAPTER 3
Social-Emotional Factors for the Gifted and Talented 23

CHAPTER 4
Twice-Exceptional Learners 35

CHAPTER 5
Grouping and Acceleration Options for Gifted Students 45

CHAPTER 6
Differentiating Curriculum, Assessment, and Instruction for Gifted Learners 55

References 73

About the Authors 83

INTRODUCTION

Intentionally Teaching Gifted Learners

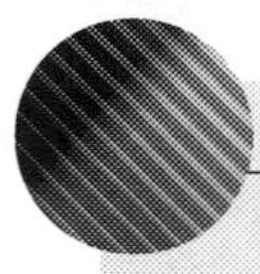

DRIVING QUESTION

Why should teachers intentionally teach gifted learners?

The term *gifted*, when associated with students or a person, often elicits feelings of superiority or negative, elitist connotations. We even considered writing this book using other terms, such as *high-potential*, *high-ability*, or *advanced*. However, we decided to keep and use the term *gifted* to maintain consistency and clarity. Throughout this book, we hope to explain why teachers need to pay attention to these students and why the term *gifted* should instead engender feelings of hope and positivity.

Although there is no universally accepted definition for *giftedness*, the National Association for Gifted Children (NAGC, 2018) supported the following:

> Students with gifts and talents perform—or have the capability to perform—at higher levels compared to others of the same age, experience, and environment in one or more

DOI: 10.4324/9781003235330-1

domains. They require modification(s) to their educational experience(s) to learn and realize their potential. Student[s] with gifts and talents:

- come from all racial, ethnic, and cultural populations, as well as all economic strata;
- require sufficient access to appropriate learning opportunities to realize their potential;
- can have learning and processing disorders that require specialized intervention and accommodation;
- need support and guidance to develop socially and emotionally as well as in their areas of talent; and
- require varied services based on their changing needs. (p. 1)

For many in gifted education, a major concern is the lack of coursework for preservice teachers about the unique needs of high-potential students. Although gifted students have individual strengths and weaknesses, they all deserve to learn every day in their classrooms. Their teachers must understand how to challenge them and push them to reach their potential, as they may become the leaders of the future. Statistically, teachers will likely encounter many of these students throughout their teaching careers.

This book is intended to help teachers—as committed, resourceful, yet very busy educators—learn about gifted students and how to engage them in learning that is stimulating, challenging, and motivating. Each chapter is organized around a *driving question* with *learning targets* that teachers will need to know in order to answer and take action on these important questions. The end of each chapter includes:

- **Reflection Questions:** These questions will help teachers think critically about each chapter's learning targets and how what they have learned relates to the students they will encounter, no matter what grade level or subject area taught.
- **Opportunities for Practice:** These easy-to-implement ideas and examples will help teachers create learning opportunities for advanced learners.

Extended resources for each chapter may also be found at https://www.Taylor & Francis Group.com/Gifted-Education-and-Gifted-Students-Resources. aspx. These Online Resources include lesson examples, tables and figures, and resources for further research, which will help teachers continue to add to their toolbox to guide advanced learners to excel.

In Chapter 1, we will review what researchers know about gifted children regarding intelligence, creativity, and identification. Chapter 2 will examine why educators must understand gifted students' ethnic, cultural, and socioeconomic backgrounds. Chapter 3 will examine the factors that can enhance or inhibit a student's journey to developing gifts into talents. Chapter 4 will help teachers understand twice-exceptional learners, their lived experience in classrooms, and how educators can best support them within gifted services. We will then explore the ideal classroom environment to foster advanced learning in Chapter 5, including grouping strategies and programming options for optimal student growth. Lastly, in Chapter 6, we will cover assessment techniques, teaching strategies, and curricular modifications that will help teachers work smarter, not harder, in planning and instruction for talented children.

We, the authors, each have more than 20 years of experience in gifted education, and still we question how we can do better for our gifted learners every day. We strive to discover more about how these students learn best and to develop innovative practices that will help them realize the depth to which they are capable of learning. These children are qualitatively different from other learners in your classroom. They need the same attention you would give special education students—they are just on the other side of the bell curve.

CHAPTER 1

Gifted Learners: Research, Theories, and Models

DRIVING QUESTION

What key philosophies, theories, models, and research support education for gifted learners?

LEARNING TARGETS

- What specific research-based models exist to explain gifted learners?
- What is known about intelligence that can help gifted learners?
- What theories and research concerning creativity apply to gifted learners?
- How do educators identify gifted learners for school programs?

In order to teach high-ability students, educators first have to better understand them. This chapter will summarize the work of Gagné (2015) and Renzulli (2012), along with research findings about

DOI: 10.4324/9781003235330-2

advanced curriculum. Additionally, some background from the field of intelligence will set the stage for the remainder of the book. These theories and models should guide teachers in their practice with advanced learners.

Research-Based Models

Gagné's (2015) Differentiating Model of Giftedness and Talent clearly distinguishes gifts (those things people are naturally born with) from talents (gifts that have been systematically developed). Intrapersonal and environmental catalysts act within the model to either help or hinder the development of gifts into talents. Additionally, Gagné included chance as a factor in talent development. Teachers have many roles within this model. They can provide an environment conducive to this developmental process as well as opportunities for students to explore new activities or programs. They can also help students better understand themselves and learn to manage their behaviors in a positive way. Conversely, teachers can also hinder the development of talent by stifling students' ability to develop their gifts.

Renzulli (2012) used a Three-Ring model to explain giftedness. One ring contains high cognitive ability, another contains creativity, and the last contains task commitment (i.e., determination, willpower, perseverance). Gifted behaviors occur within the overlap of all three rings. Renzulli believed the word *gifted* should be used as an adjective to describe behaviors, like a "gifted mathematician," instead of as a noun. Renzulli felt that educators should not label students as *gifted* or *not gifted*, but instead should examine behaviors that manifest as gifted and encourage the growth of these behaviors. To do this, teachers should focus on teaching creativity and encouraging task commitment. Students should be given time and space to explore a particular subject or skill. Teachers also need to engage students by using teaching methods like inductive instruction (i.e., knowledge gained from investigation and exploration with topics), enriching activities that challenge students, and a learning environment that encourages intellectual pursuit.

Intelligence

Intelligence is often measured using standardized tests. Various aspects of intelligence may be measured depending on the assessment and how many dimensions are utilized. The Wechsler Intelligence Scale for Children (WISC-V; Wechsler, 2014) is a common assessment in schools. It measures the verbal (vocabulary and comprehension) and the performance (matrix reasoning and picture completion) aspects of intelligence. Because it takes 65–80 minutes to administer, sometimes an even shorter assessment, like the Naglieri Nonverbal Ability Test (NNAT; Naglieri, 2018), will be given to determine which students should qualify for gifted programming. Because the NNAT is a nonverbal assessment, it has been used to eliminate assessment bias with English language learners (ELLs) and students from diverse cultural and economic backgrounds. Children are asked to solve a series of increasingly difficult puzzles, which yields a nonverbal cognitive ability score. Another common assessment is the Cognitive Abilities Test (CogAT), which includes a battery of verbal, quantitative, and nonverbal test items.

Research indicates the importance of a teacher's perception of a student's intelligence. This perception links to teacher expectations, student academic identity development, and school inequities (Hatt, 2012). Teachers' pedagogical practices and discourse with students will be influenced by their beliefs about the intelligence of each student. Expectations are often higher when a teacher believes a student is smarter (Sternberg, 2007). Students begin to develop an identity as either "smart" or "dumb" in school based on these pedagogical practices and discourse occurring in their classrooms (Hatt, 2012). School inequities, such as limited access to advanced coursework and teachers rewarding students who are seen as more intelligent, must be vigilantly prevented.

The bell curve of intelligence is a normal curve, meaning there are as many people on the right (high intelligence) as there are on the left (low intelligence). Statistically, in any given general education classroom, there are just as many students with high intelligence as there are with cognitive impairment.

Creativity

Creativity is an important part of gifted education. Some definitions of *gifted* include creativity as a dimension (Renzulli, 2012). Creative production helps to bring genius ideas into the world. Sometimes teachers think of creativity as a "fuzzy" concept that they cannot define, which makes it difficult to teach or incorporate into classes. In fact, the creative process can be explained in eight stages that are easily reproduced in class activities (Sawyer, 2012):

1. **Find the problem:** Students must identify an ill-defined problem that has many possible solutions/answers and is not easily solved.
2. **Acquire knowledge relevant to the problem:** Students must practice before they can create by learning everything about the problem.
3. **Gather all potentially related information:** Often creativity happens when seemingly unrelated information is connected in a new way.
4. **Incubation:** Allow time for the unconscious mind to process all of the information and search for new combinations and creative solutions to the problem.
5. **Generate a large variety of ideas:** Create a conclusive list of potential solutions to the problem, based on all knowledge gained (sometimes called brainstorming).
6. **Combine ideas in unexpected ways:** Encourage students to construct combinations from different domains or disciplines to generate original ideas to solve the problem.
7. **Select the best ideas:** Have students carefully evaluate each idea to determine its merit in solving the problem and then choose the strongest possibilities.
8. **Externalize the idea:** Students can share their solution with others digitally (e.g., website, blog, application), concretely (e.g., poster, display board, mobile, model, etc.), or in an entirely new way.

By allowing students to complete the creative process in the classroom, educators teach students that creativity can be developed and that students are capable of generating new ideas.

The learning environment also plays an important role in student learning and students' ability to produce creatively (Beghetto, Kaufman, & Baer, 2015). In order to support standards-based learning and creativity simultaneously, teachers need to send a positive message that makes students feel supported and motivated to learn and create. Teachers can do this by integrating students' interests and passions into lessons. Teachers should give students freedom to generate messy ideas and take intellectual risks in the classroom. Students can focus on their individual improvement of goals, which encourages them to only compete against themselves and not worry about how they measure up to others. This will also help students take pride in their work, solutions, and ideas (Beghetto et al., 2015).

Identifying Gifted Learners

Many theoretical and psychological factors should be considered when determining how students will be identified for gifted services. Categorizing students as *gifted* or *not gifted* is an arduous task wrought with complexities and a few problems. Many programs start with a referral process. Assessing students can be costly and time-consuming, so referrals allow the school to pinpoint which students need a closer look. Often teachers and/or parents are asked to refer students for gifted testing. Sometimes community member referrals, peer referrals, and self-nomination are also encouraged. Another option is to screen all students of a particular group (e.g., all kindergarteners might take the NNAT). Screening all students may eliminate some of the bias associated with nominating students. A more inclusive approach that allows equitable access to gifted programming is always recommended. One approach is to use multiple types of data in the initial screening phase (see Figure 1).

When considering students for gifted programs, educators must ensure that instruments and protocols include both qualitative and

Gifted Program Identification Profile

Student Name (Last, First): ____________________ ID Number: ______
D.O.B.: ________
School: ______________________ Current Grade: _________ ❑ Male ❑ Female
Previously Identified G/T: ❑ Y ❑ N School District: _________
City/State: _________
Referral: ❑ Educator ❑ Parent ❑ Other: ____________________________

Nomination	Was Student Enrolled in G/T Program at Another District?	Grades Top 10% Semester Avg.	Teacher Input		Parent Input		Student Input	
	❑ Yes ❑ No	ELAR Math	Leadership		Leadership		Math	
			Creativity		Creativity		Reading	
			Reading		Reading		Interview	
			Math		Math			
			Science		Science			

Students must meet two out of the five district-established criteria listed above to move into the screening phase.

Parent Notification of DNQ (Does Not Qualify):____________ (date)

Screening	Achievement			Aptitude		Portfolio/Products	
	Language: ❑ English ❑ Other: _________			Test Name: Level:	Language: ❑ English ❑ Other: _________	Language: ❑ English ❑ Other: _________	
	Content	**Test/Level**	**Score**	**Results***		**Content**	**Score**
	Reading					ELA	
	Social Studies					Humanities	
	Math					Math	
	Science					Science	

Students must meet the district-established criteria for their current grade.

* In this space, test administrators can write the results of the subtests of whichever aptitude assessment was given.

Figure 1. Screening example with multiple types of data.

Quantitative Data	0 Points	1 Point	2 Points	3 Points
Aptitude	Less than 79th percentile	80th–89th percentile	90th–95th percentile	96th–99th percentile
Verbal				
Quantitative				
Nonverbal				
Total				
Achievement/Grades	0—Bottom 80% of class	1—Top 20% of class	2 —Top 10% of class	3—Top 5% of class
Reading				
Math				
Qualitative Data	0 points—Less than 79th percentile	1 point—80th–89th percentile	2 points—90th–95th percentile	3 points—96th–99th percentile
Leadership				
Creativity				
Teacher Inventory				
Parent Inventory				
Interview				
Additional Data				
Qualitative Total				
Free and Reduced Lunch	No = 0 points		Yes = 2 points	
Qualifies for Special Education	No = 0 points		Yes = 2 points	
English Language Learner	No = 0 points		Yes = 2 points	
Total for All Categories				

Figure 2. Gifted identification matrix.

quantitative data collection. Many quantitative assessments are available to measure various constructs (e.g., subject areas, cognitive ability, creativity). These are often valid and reliable, but still contain measurement error. Qualitative data may lower this error by adding flexibility for both the examiner and examinee (Kettler & Margot, 2015). These data can be collected through interviews, portfolios, and performance task assessments. Once all data are collected, no one source of data should be weighted more heavily than others. The use of cut scores (e.g., students must score at least 125 on a cognitive ability test to qualify for a gifted program) is not considered best practice. One way to make decisions about gifted placement based on the collection of data is through the use of a matrix. Each piece of data can be given a number of points, and then the total points can be added up to make a decision. Points can be added for students with disabilities, twice-exceptional (2e) students, students from poverty, or students who are otherwise disadvantaged. Figure 2 is an example of this type of matrix.

Perhaps most importantly, there must be alignment between identification procedures and gifted program services. Teachers must establish and then deconstruct the goals of the gifted program or course, and then look for students who are capable of achieving those goals. Likely giftedness should be identified in increasingly domain-specific ways as children get older. As schools start to offer advanced courses in specific subject areas, they should seek students who are performing at those levels or have the potential to perform at those levels in that particular subject/domain (Kettler & Margot, 2015). In other words, if looking for students to participate in an advanced mathematics course, it would not be prudent to use their verbal skills/scores. Instead educators would take a closer look at how students are currently performing in math and/or their potential ability to do well in an advanced mathematics course.

Reflection Questions

- What can you do in a classroom to help students be more task-committed?
- How can you incorporate the creative process into something you will teach in your class?
- How do you think the two identification profiles (Figures 1 and 2) would work in a school or district? What challenges can you foresee? What can you do to help alleviate those challenges?

Opportunities for Practice

- Create or modify a lesson that will encourage students to work harder on a particular set of standards.
- Create an activity for a class that has students complete the steps of the creative process using standards you teach (see Online Resources for an example).
- Develop or modify a profile page (with multiple pieces of qualitative and quantitative data) for identifying gifted learners that would fit a district or school.

CHAPTER 2

Underrepresented Populations in Gifted Education

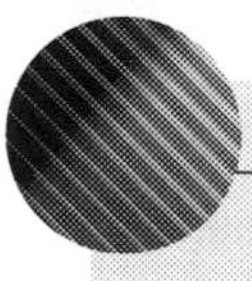

DRIVING QUESTION

What role does culture, ethnicity, or socioeconomic status play in the identification and instruction process?

LEARNING TARGETS

- How are students in underrepresented populations identified for services?
- What are best practices for ensuring equitable identification and programming for traditionally underrepresented gifted populations?

Identification of Underrepresented Populations

Students from certain populations have been underidentified for gifted programs for many years, which leads to a greater disparity in

DOI: 10.4324/9781003235330-3

the achievement gap. Low-income and ethnically diverse students have a long history of underrepresentation in gifted programs at schools (Peters & Engerrand, 2016). Researchers have tried to address underrepresentation by investigating identification practices (McBee, 2006). However, few schools and districts have succeeded in matching the gifted population demographics to the overall socioeconomic and ethnically diverse population (Kettler & Margot, 2015). For example, if 40% of a district's students are on free and reduced lunch, then 40% of its students identified as gifted should also be on free and reduced lunch. The gifted population demographics should mirror the overall student population (Texas Education Agency, 2009).

Most school districts use ability or achievement assessments as part of their identification practices. Unfortunately, underrepresented populations perform lower on these assessments than their more privileged classmates (Ford, 2010). This is not due to the capabilities of ethnically diverse students but instead to the lack of resources available to them. The idea that giftedness manifests as an already developed phenomenon, as demonstrated by high achievement in school and on assessments, is also problematic and needs to be reexamined (Olszewski-Kubilius & Clarenbach, 2012). Processes used to identify students for gifted programs must seek out students who have the *potential* to perform at the highest levels. If educators want to increase equity in gifted programs, they must find ways to be more inclusive in their identification practices (Siegle et al., 2016).

When seeking more equitable methods of identification to gifted programs, school districts must consider the fact that teachers do not refer some student populations as often for screening (Ford, 2010). Many teachers struggle to understand how giftedness manifests differently in low-income and ethnically diverse students (Speirs Neumeister, Adams, Pierce, Cassady, & Dixon, 2007). For example, students living in poverty may express their high abilities differently (Olszewski-Kubilius & Corwith, 2018). These students often obtain lower grades in academic courses than their higher socioeconomic status (SES) peers. They are also less likely to take Advanced Placement (AP) classes or perform well on AP exams. Children living in poverty often attend schools with fewer resources and funding, have access to less nutritious food, and have limited access to enrichment opportunities outside of school.

In another study, both high- and low-income students were asked to describe barriers they felt impeded their academic success (Cross, Frazier, Kim, & Cross, 2018). The low-income students reported major impediments in their school environment resulting from chaotic systems and lack of academic and technology resources. Similarly, Leu et al. (2015) found that students at schools with a majority of low-SES populations had fewer skills in technology due to a lack of access to the tools and training required. In contrast, the high-income students in the Cross et al. (2018) study reported very different impediments to their learning, such as slow Internet, slow updates on educational software, and peer issues in their regular classes. Clearly, high-income students had much greater access to rich resources in their classrooms. Often children from underrepresented populations have teachers who are not equipped to identify their potential or develop curriculum appropriate for this development of talent (Olszewski-Kubilius & Clarenbach, 2012).

In short, in order to identify more diverse populations, including low-SES students, schools need to employ more qualitative identification methods to increase access to gifted programs. Equity in gifted identification practices requires educators to think differently about ability, potential, and opportunity so that all students have access to excel academically.

Best Practices for Equitable Identification and Programming

The use of universal screening and local norms is one recommended strategy to shrink the achievement gap between underrepresented students and their peers (Plucker & Peters, 2018; Worrell & Dixson, 2018). Universal screening gives every student an initial opportunity to qualify for advanced academic programs through some form of testing or observation instrument, and can eliminate teacher referral bias. The Slocumb-Payne Teacher Perception Inventory (Slocumb, Payne, &

Williams, 2018) was developed to identify gifted students from diverse backgrounds. Additionally, recommendations include the use of local norms instead of national norms (Plucker & Peters, 2018; Worrell & Dixson, 2018). Local norms ensure that students are only being compared to their school or district peers, improving the chances of access to gifted programs for diverse populations (Plucker & Peters, 2018). Additionally, district employees need to intentionally look for students from poverty and other underrepresented populations who have the potential for performing at higher academic levels. Districts should seek out these students in their early years and provide academic challenge and psychosocial supports (e.g., perseverance, mindset, etc.) as soon as possible. When school districts implement these identification procedures with intentionality, students experience upward mobility and more success in advanced academics (Loveless, 2016).

Worrell and Dixson (2018) recommended making gifted programs more attractive to underrepresented students by recruiting these students in groups instead of individually and purposefully making the gifted courses more culturally relevant for them. By recruiting students in groups, educators decrease the chance that a single student will feel isolated from an identified peer group, and students are more likely to feel a sense of belonging. Educators must also consider that students' ethnic identity is important to them and does not always match their academic identity (Worrell, 2014). Culturally relevant pedagogy in gifted classes helps students from diverse backgrounds to feel more comfortable. Because the United States has a long history of racism and discrimination (Kneebone, 2014), educators must address the belief systems of ethnically diverse and disadvantaged student groups. One recommendation is to encourage and celebrate ways students can engage in cultural heritage enrichment opportunities (Worrell & Dixson, 2018).

Teachers and Role Models

Targeted professional learning that helps teachers understand the lives of diverse students is a crucial component of increasing equity and access to gifted programs. In order to identify and better serve economically disadvantaged and ethnically diverse students, teachers must understand the unique characteristics and needs of these children (Olszewski-Kubilius & Clarenbach, 2012). Teachers should also receive training on the strategies that have proven successful for diverse learners. For instance, districts and/or schools could have teachers participate in guided study groups using programs such as the HiCapPLUS Professional Learning Modules (Office of Superintendent of Public Instruction, n.d.). Because this learning is current and customizable, districts can easily implement these modules to improve advanced academic programming for diverse learners.

Providing role models from underrepresented groups is an additional way to help diverse students feel welcome in gifted courses (Worrell & Dixson, 2018). When schools intentionally staff these role models in academic supports, such as tutoring, supplemental instruction, and technology labs, students are more likely to feel comfortable asking questions and getting help. For example, Evans (2015) found that 80% of students from underrepresented groups chose not to participate in gifted courses because they felt they would be a minority within a minority group. Instructional coaches who reflect the students' race or ethnic background can help these students feel more included. Additionally, seeing academically successful persons from similar backgrounds can serve as a crucial motivator for students from underrepresented groups (Worrell & Dixson, 2018).

For at-risk students, the role of individuals invested in their well-being and academic success is especially important (Olszewski-Kubilius & Steenbergen-Hu, 2017). A caring educator or mentor can help develop a student's emerging talent, encourage the student through adversity, and provide new opportunities and ideas. By providing a supportive presence, these educators and mentors can help students persevere through adversity and reach their long-term goals (Olszewski-Kubilius & Clarenbach, 2012).

Gifted Programs That Include Equalizing Components

Parents often seek learning opportunities outside of school programs to enrich their gifted children's lives (Olszewski-Kubilius & Clarenbach, 2012). Although these opportunities may serve to develop children's talents, the majority of these programs have high costs. Access to such enrichment opportunities is another barrier to underrepresented populations. To address this disparity, school districts can design and offer additional opportunities through their gifted programming to their most vulnerable students. For instance, supplemental programs that provide added time in academic areas (e.g., math, science, language arts) with experts teaching the domain (e.g., biology teacher, math teacher) have been shown to positively affect student achievement (Olszewski-Kubilius & Steenbergen-Hu, 2017). These programs also better prepare participating students for advanced coursework in high school. This kind of subject-area enrichment appears to reduce the gap between the advantaged and disadvantaged student.

Gifted programs can also incorporate higher level thinking and problem solving opportunities for economically disadvantaged and ethnically diverse students (VanTassel-Baska, 2018). Strategies that have proven successful include questions that foster deeper thinking, collaborative problem solving around real-world issues, and academic scaffolds that allow students to advance their thinking to higher levels.

Finally, to increase the likelihood that diverse students will be successful in gifted programs and advanced learning opportunities, schools must intentionally develop students' psychosocial skills (Worrell & Dixson, 2018). Woo, Bang, Cauley, and Choi (2017) found that direct instruction in psychosocial skills significantly impacted the overall well-being of underrepresented students. Additional neurological and educational research indicates that psychosocial factors are an important part of a student's success or failure in academic environments (Olenchak, 2009). Although it remains unclear which factors are most important, programs that help students with self-regulation, task commitment, risk-taking, and interpersonal competence equip diverse learners to be more successful as their coursework becomes increasingly difficult (Worrell, 2009).

Reflection Questions

- Research a school or district to find out what it is doing to identify highly capable students from diverse backgrounds. Does the coursework match the ways these students are identified and meet these students' needs?
- What professional development do you feel a school needs in order to better develop the talents of diverse groups of students? What do teachers need to know and understand about low-SES and minority students?

Opportunities for Practice

- Create an afterschool club or organization that would be an enrichment opportunity for diverse learners. This could also be a lunch group meeting. In what ways can you specifically address these learners' lack of experiences/resources?
- Develop an agenda for professional development for a school or district that focuses on inclusive practices for diverse gifted learners.

CHAPTER 3

Social-Emotional Factors for the Gifted and Talented

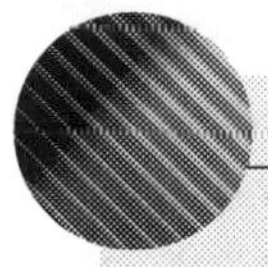

DRIVING QUESTION

What social-emotional factors enhance or inhibit the development of gifts and talents?

LEARNING TARGETS

- What skills and attitudes do teachers need to foster the social-emotional growth of gifted learners?
- What interventions associated with social-emotional factors have proven effective?
- What educational factors inhibit academic development in gifted learners?
- What counseling and guidance strategies can facilitate gifted learners' development?

Cognitive, Affective, Developmental, and Behavioral Factors

Gifted education research suggests that gifted children can be vulnerable to social-emotional issues (VanTassel-Baska, 2009). NAGC's (2009) position statement on the topic states:

DOI: 10.4324/9781003235330-4

> Gifted youth deserve attention to their well-being and to their universal and unique developmental experiences—beyond academic and/or talent performance or non-performance. Gifted education programs, teachers, administrators, and school counselors can and should intentionally, purposefully, and proactively nurture socio-emotional development in these students. Gifted children and adolescents are not only developing cognitively; they are also developing socially and emotionally and in career awareness. Even cognitive development and academic experiences have social and emotional implications. (para. 2)

Teachers need to consider the whole child, not just cognitive development, when making educational decisions about gifted students. In some cases, gifted students may differ greatly from their classmates and age-mates in psychological and social characteristics. By paying attention to these differences and supporting advanced learners when issues arise, teachers can better nurture their academic abilities.

Some gifted children are high achievers who seek to develop their talents in specific domains of interest (Cross, 2016), and this can cause anxiety (Gaesser, 2018). Additionally, gifted students often must learn to cope with asynchronous development and social status issues (Cross, 2016). Asynchronous development means that various facets of gifted students' development (academic, social, emotional, or physical) may be uneven and can make them vulnerable. For example, students who are cognitively advanced for their age may still struggle with physical tasks like handwriting or coordination.

To help students develop healthy lives and promote their gifts and talents, educators must pay attention to their social-emotional development and help them acquire the psychosocial skills needed to perform at such high academic levels (Rinn & Majority, 2018). Because social-emotional development occurs over a student's lifetime (Coleman & Cross, 2005), schools must ensure that teachers and counselors are paying attention to this development.

Some gifted children struggle with making and keeping same-age friends (Freeman, 2006). A preference for complex thought and ideas can cause problems with their social relationships and make gifted children feel isolated (Coleman & Cross, 2005). Access to like-minded peers through ability or cluster grouping has been shown to positively foster these relationships (Vogl & Preckel, 2014).

Giftedness can be a burden or a boon depending on how children respond to their environment and adversity. On one hand, having advanced cognitive ability will likely allow students to problem solve, feel in control, and analyze complex situations (Peterson, 2012). Intelligence is also linked to resilience (Higgins, 1994) and high standards (Rinn & Majority, 2018). However, gifted child may struggle with the expectations of others, fear of risk-taking, and stress related to overcommitment (Peterson, 2009).

Effective Social-Emotional Interventions

Teachers are often the first to identify social-emotional issues and can help students learn to cope with these challenges using an affective curriculum. An affective curriculum proactively helps students learn about social and emotional issues and how to better handle them. This information might be presented through guest speakers, small-group discussions, counselor-led conversations, or writing groups. The affective curriculum should be created with children's development in mind (VanTassel-Baska, 2009). Children's needs, both social-emotional and cognitive, change as they age, and these changes should be considered. This type of curriculum should help gifted students understand themselves and how their personalities, aptitudes, and interests contribute to the people they are (VanTassel-Baska, 2009). By helping students self-assess, teachers empower them to be better advocates for their own learning needs. Teachers might use a tool to help children get to know themselves better and share their interests, such as Renzulli's (1997) Interest-A-Lyzer.

Bibliotherapy

Educators can also implement affective lessons through bibliotherapy, a dynamic interaction that can happen between a reader and a book, resulting in deeper understanding of one's personality, adjustment, and growth. Students can learn to better understand themselves by identifying with characters from stories. Halsted's (2009) *Some of My Best Friends Are Books* integrates bibliotherapy into the curriculum in developmentally appropriate ways. Halsted explained how both intellectual and emotional growth can be supported by reading and discussing well-chosen books. Books are recommended based on a child's stage of development and age (see Online Resources for more). Sometimes children have a difficult time discussing their own experiences and emotions but might be able to work through similar situations that a character faces. Teachers can use small groups and targeted questions to help students explore their emotional responses to a book. The book must also be intellectually stimulating and appropriately challenging. Teachers should lead open-ended discussions and foster a culture of respect for others to encourage student participation and growth.

Cinematherapy

As an extension of bibliotherapy, gifted students may benefit from cinematherapy through the guided viewing of a film in which the characters show gifted traits or deal with circumstances associated with giftedness (Kangas, Cook, & Rule, 2017). Newton (1995) proposed that movies may appeal to visual learners more than books because movies involve multiple senses. Gifted adolescents may be more receptive to discussing sensitive topics through popular films because of their links to contemporary culture.

When viewing films with gifted learners, Hébert and Speirs Neumeister (2001) suggested that facilitators:

- familiarize themselves with the film's content and the characters' emotions, attitudes, and beliefs;
- introduce the film by explaining what prompted them to use the movie for discussion purposes;
- help students identify with the movie's characters;
- respond to students' comments and concerns throughout the viewing;

- develop a menu of questions that encourage students to share their experiences; and
- design follow-up activities that allow students to process their feelings through artistic expressions, writing activities, role-playing, and creative problem solving.

Service Learning

When gifted students feel disconnected from the goals of the school, they are likely to underachieve. Service learning projects that involve student choice, interests, and concerns have been shown to reverse underachievement in gifted youth by giving students a sense of ownership (Bruce-Davis & Chancey, 2012). Engaging students in service-learning projects can also help to increase their sense of belonging as they become more aware of larger social or moral issues and develop a sense of concern for the welfare of others. The implementation of service-learning projects within the curriculum holds the potential to address gifted students' affective needs; it provides students an opportunity to learn about their communities, interact and engage with diverse populations, exercise empathy, and develop intense care for others (Beason-Manes, 2018). Not only can service learning help gifted students seek creative solutions to challenges in our society, but it also has been shown to help gifted students stretch toward self-actualization (Terry, 2008).

Encourage Creative Practices

It may be possible to enhance students' giftedness by teaching them creative practices. Gotlieb, Hyde, Immordino-Yang, and Kaufman (2016) suggested including the development of reflective social-emotional skills in curriculum. Too often schools focus on tasks that make "high demands on externally focused attention," such as listening to lectures, completing worksheets, taking notes, or working in laboratories (p. 24). In addition to these tasks that require intense concentration, opportunities need to be given for introspective tasks like reflection, connection building, and personal meaning making. By encouraging intellectual curiosity, teachers can help students make connections across time and disciplines needed for innovative thinking.

School Messages

Schools must also examine the messages they sends to students. The goals and objectives of a school have been found to influence the social and emotional development of advanced learners, especially in regard to students' perception of emotional safety, acceptance of individual differences, and the relationships between students and teachers (Eddles-Hirsch, Vialle, Rogers, & McCormick, 2010). Schools that intentionally provide social-emotional support of affective needs may provide better learning environments for gifted learners. Using an affective curriculum that offers perspective and guidance on developmental challenges (e.g., bullying, developing identity, autonomy) can be very helpful to students (Peterson, 2009).

Grow Emotional Intelligence

Many researchers believe the conception of intelligence needs to be expanded to include a person's ability to experience, express, and regulate emotions (Mayer, Caruso, & Salovey, 2016; Zeidner & Matthews, 2017). Mayer and Salovey "proposed that emotionally intelligent people (a) perceive emotions accurately, (b) use emotions to accurately facilitate thought, (c) understand emotions and emotional meanings, and (d) manage emotions in themselves and others" (as cited in Mayer et al., 2016, p. 291). Mayer et al. (2016) also developed a theoretical framework that helps educators understand and assess a person's emotional intelligence. Educators can use this framework to develop K–12 curriculum to support the growth of emotional intelligence (VanTassel-Baska, 2009). For example, Mayer et al. (2016) outlined the importance of a person's ability to problem solve in order to understand another person's emotions, predict future emotional behaviors, and manage the emotions of others. One goal in classroom activities is to help students "prioritize thinking by directing attention according to present feelings" (p. 294).

High emotional intelligence may be beneficial to gifted students (Matthews, Lin, Zeidner, & Roberts, 2017). This ability to navigate the emotional world may enhance students' talent development as they progress through school: "High emotionally intelligent youth have been reported to have more positive relationships, are less likely to engage in risk-taking behaviors, experience fewer emotional symptoms, and perform better academically" (p. 166). Because these students can better evaluate, process, and cope with the behavior of those around them and their own actions (Mayer et al., 2016), they are able to more successfully enjoy social interactions in and out of school. Increasing emotional intelligence may have the potential to protect gifted students' resilience and adaptation in school as they develop their subject-area knowledge and cope with academic stressors (Matthews et al., 2017).

Extracurricular Activities

Extracurricular activities can help gifted students to identify their talent areas and develop their abilities with other talented peers through competition, challenge, and enjoyment. Olszewski-Kubilius and Lee (2004) surveyed 247 gifted students in grades 5–11 who attended a summer enrichment program. Students were asked about the kinds of activities they participated in both inside and outside of school. The top two activities were sports and music; more than 70% of students participated in these activities.

Gifted learners can benefit from participating in extracurricular activities focused on their talents in the form of competitions and contests. Competitions can provide a learning environment that stresses academic challenge and is often difficult to recreate in the classroom (Ozturk & Debelak, 2008). Competitions and contests can foster the development of productive attitudes and work habits and can nurture emotional and psychological growth. Meeting students from other schools and interacting with judges and sponsors enhance interpersonal skills. Time management skills are also developed, including punctuality, following directions, and responsible behavior (Karnes & Riley, 1997).

Underachievement and Motivation

The discrepancy between what gifted students are capable of and how they are performing academically sometimes indicates underachievement. Parents and teachers often expect that gifted children will do well in school, which leads some students to withdraw and underachieve (Cross, 2016). These underachieving gifted students often report lower satisfaction with teachers and school, and value education less than their achieving peers. These students also do not appear motivated by or see value in grades. Research indicates that lack of academic challenge is almost certainly a part of the problem (Snyder & Linnenbrink-Garcia, 2013). Often the term *gifted* is associated with a fixed set of traits and abilities, which may shape these students' beliefs in themselves as able to outperform their peers. If this belief is challenged as school becomes more difficult, students may begin to doubt their gifted label.

Because self-worth is influenced by success or failure at tasks, students may begin to form a negative self-worth around academics if they feel they are not performing well enough (Snyder & Linnenbrink-Garcia, 2013). Once students' academic self-worth is threatened, they begin to develop maladaptive coping mechanisms, including not trying. By not trying, these students believe they are both protecting themselves from failure and preventing their true ability from being measured. Students may also disconnect with academics and devalue teacher feedback to protect themselves from feelings of negative self-worth. Another theory suggests that as school gets harder, underachieving gifted students begin to feel that the cost (time and effort) is too great. Unfortunately, decreasing academic challenge can have negative effects and cause underachievement to worsen (Snyder & Linnenbrink-Garcia, 2013).

One suggestion to combat underachievement is to create a new narrative around the gifted label when students are young. Instead of leading students to believe that giftedness is a fixed trait associated with high intelligence and ease in school, teachers can help students to understand that hard work is required and all students struggle at some time.

Schools can also provide interventions aimed at reversing the maladaptive coping mechanisms to help students develop more adaptive behaviors. Interventions may be more impactful if they are timed well and used during periods of transition for students (Snyder & Linnenbrink-Garcia, 2013). Educators can carefully monitor students to determine if there is a positive academic shift during the intervention. When possible, getting parents and counselors involved may also be helpful.

Motivation is an important factor when teachers are trying to encourage student engagement. Both personal and environmental factors contribute to a students' academic motivation. The question becomes: How can teachers leverage these factors to increase a student's ability to persevere in a given task? Task commitment is crucial to gifted productivity. Renzulli (2012) even included task commitment as a part of the equation that yields gifted behaviors. Educators must try to match the academic difficulty with student ability in that domain/subject area. This match provides an optimal environment for students to feel engaged and motivated. Additionally, whenever possible, teachers must allow students to choose tasks that are valuable and interesting to them. This gives students additional impetus to engage.

Counseling and Guidance Strategies

Although there is evidence that some gifted children are actually better adjusted than their peers regarding their psychological state (Martin, Burns, & Schonlau, 2010), some gifted children need support from a counselor or psychologist in order to fully develop their talents. Loneliness should be considered during counseling, as it can put students at a higher risk for adverse psychological symptoms (Ogurlu, Yalin, & Yavuz Birben, 2018). Some researchers believe that loneliness may be a result of social skill deficits (Foley-Nicpon et al., 2017; Malcolm, Jensen-Campbell, Rex-Lear, & Waldrip, 2006). Other studies have shown that anxiety in gifted children can negatively impact academic success (Martin et al., 2010). Therefore, anxiety should also be considered by counselors working with gifted students.

Fortunately, there are intervention strategies that have proven effective in helping gifted children thrive despite these psychological issues. For example, Foley-Nicpon et al. (2017) found that a 2-week summer enrichment program teaching social skills and talent development improved the quality of friendships. During the enrichment program, a lunchtime group participated in modeling of their own and other students' behaviors in video recordings. The groups would then discuss the social interactions, including what worked and did not work well. Another group of researchers (Doss & Bloom, 2018) implemented a 30-day unit on mindfulness to help students alleviate stress and anxiety. By guiding students through the process of daily meditation and encouraging students to apply these techniques in their daily lives, teachers helped some of the adolescents to begin using mindfulness exercises to successfully tackle problems.

Discussion groups are another way students can make connections and normalize their feelings and concerns. The facilitator should resist the urge to offer solutions, but instead allow ideas to organically form from the group participants. Teachers can encourage students to listen carefully to each other and validate the other participants' feelings. It can be helpful to inform parents about these groups so they can continue the conversation at home. The groups should be small, with no more than 6–8 students when possible (Peterson, Betts, & Bradley, 2009). Groups can decide on topics for discussion so that students take ownership of the process. Facilitators should ask open-ended questions, keeping the discussion focused but flexible. These group discussions can help gifted children learn to discuss and constructively process their emotions.

Reflection Questions

- Have you known students with high academic potential who underachieve in school? What do you think a school could do to better support this type of learner?

- How important is students' emotional intelligence to their academic growth? How can educators increase students' emotional intelligence?
- What counseling strategies work with gifted students?
- What extracurricular options are available for advanced learners in your district, region, or state? What can you do to make these options accessible to the students in a classroom or school? How would students benefit from these opportunities?

Opportunities for Practice

- Create an intervention to help underachieving students. How will you know if the intervention is successful?
- Develop a lesson incorporating your standards that encourages the growth of students' emotional intelligence.
- Think of one specific psychological symptom you might encounter in gifted learners (e.g., anxiety, fear of failure, perfectionism) and create a plan to help students cope with their feelings and thrive in the classroom environment.

CHAPTER 4

Twice-Exceptional Learners

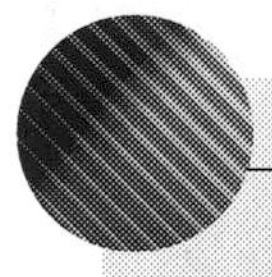

DRIVING QUESTION

How can teachers provide a better academic challenge for their twice-exceptional learners?

LEARNING TARGETS

- What is a twice-exceptional learner?
- What are research-based best practices for instruction with these students?
- How can counselors support twice-exceptional learners?

Twice-exceptional students, who both demonstrate the potential for high academic achievement *and* are diagnosed with one or more disabilities, are often overlooked by educators (Reis, Baum, & Burke, 2014). These students are intelligent and often capable of advanced academics (with appropriate modifications). In medicine, this type of dual diagnosis would result in comorbidity, or the manifestation of a new set of behaviors and traits resulting from the two diagnoses interacting. This same phenomenon is often seen in 2e students; an entirely new set

 DOI: 10.4324/9781003235330-5

of behaviors may result from the interaction of a student's giftedness and disability. Often, these students will exhibit traits unlike those seen in other gifted students, and these traits vary depending on the individual and the diagnosis. In these students, gifted traits can mask the disability and/or the disability can mask the gifts, resulting in neither being identified by teachers. These students' test scores often do not match their grades (Foley-Nicpon, 2018). Despite the large amount of research on 2e students, some teachers still do not believe that students can both be gifted and have learning deficits (Baum, Renzulli, & Rizza, 2015).

In order to ensure that 2e students are correctly identified and placed, educators must understand their unique characteristics and needs. They must advocate for a comprehensive assessment of both conditions and for identification criteria to take into account the comorbidity challenges (Reis et al., 2014). Once identified, 2e students need access to services for both their giftedness and their disability. Neihart (2008) argued that developing their talent is the most important part of their education. Often these students need to be taught compensation strategies to help them manage their disabilities in an academically challenging environment (Baum, Schader, & Owen, 2017). Also, both teachers and 2e students need to understand the asynchronous development that often occurs with dual diagnosis. Uneven developmental rates in a child's emotional, intellectual, social, and motor skills are often confusing for both the student and teacher.

Five factors that contribute to the academic growth of 2e students are (Baum et al., 2017):

- a psychologically safe environment;
- tolerance for asynchronous behaviors;
- allowing students time without rushing or demanding;
- positive relationships with peers, faculty, and family; and
- a strength-based, talent-focused environment (p. 60).

For students who have a dual diagnosis of advanced abilities and learning challenges, opportunities to develop in their areas of strength and passion promote a positive learning environment in which they are more likely to flourish (see Table 1).

Table 1

Five Factors That Contribute to Academic Success for 2e Students

Factor*	What Does This Look Like in the Classroom?
Psychologically safe environment	• Students have freedom to make choices about their learning. • Risk-taking is encouraged and supported. • Bullying is not allowed. • Trust is supported among diverse learners. • A safe and welcoming climate helps students examine social issues and learn more about themselves.
Tolerance for asynchronous behaviors	• Teachers understand that a student may have varied levels of academic, social, emotional, and physical development that do not "match up." • Supports (e.g., text-to-speech software, motor skill modifications, assistive technology) are in place to maximize learning.
Allowing students time without rushing or demanding	• Flexible learning activities allow for varied time limits; students can transition to the next activity when finished. • Teachers help students to find a balance between completed work and "perfect" work.
Positive relationships with peers, teachers, and family	• Students receive instruction on social skills. • Students are able to work both in solitude and in groups. • There is an appreciation of diverse learners. • Students develop common goals within groups. • All students feel a sense of belonging and autonomy.
Strength-based, talent-focused environment	• Feedback is focused on effort. • Students are allowed to learn subjects they struggle with through their strengths.

*Factors are drawn from Baum et al., 2017.

Research-Based Best Practices for Twice-Exceptional Students

Educational research indicates that 2e students benefit from a strength-based approach, meaning that teachers focus on the child's strengths first and then scaffold for the disability (Baum et al., 2017). Providing choice is an important aspect of strength-based learning. With this approach, students are able to compensate for weaknesses that normally make them uncomfortable while being enticed to learn more about an area of interest. For example, a student who is both gifted and dyslexic might be allowed to write about her favorite topic, archaeology, while using a laptop with spell check. Or, a gifted student with autism spectrum disorders (ASD) who prefers working alone might be permitted to work independently on a group project, creating advanced mathematics problems about his favorite topic, dinosaurs. These students' strengths can be used as motivators. Additionally, time spent on review may be reduced, as many of these students find it boring and disengage. Teachers can use formative assessment to determine which of the targets students have already mastered and reduce their workload accordingly. By using their strengths, 2e students are allowed to create products in their areas of interest instead of feeling as though they are unsuccessful or unable to contribute in areas of weakness (Baum et al., 2017). Table 2 shares some ideas for how to use interventions in a strength-based approach. When helping 2e students socially, Foley-Nicpon (2018) suggested using four positive examples of their behaviors and then one corrected social skill. In this way, teachers can stay positive and give students hope for their social interactions while gently correcting behaviors.

Additionally, teachers can work with 2e students to help them be more flexible in their thinking processes, perhaps through simulations or debates. Students can complete performance-based assessments (see Chapter 6) with differentiated exit points (Baum et al., 2017), meaning that students have some choice or personalization in how they finalize their product. For example, a student who struggles with writing but has a vivid imagination and understanding of science concepts might create a video narrative instead of a writing assignment. Concentrating

Table 2
Interventions Used in a Strength-Based Approach

	Talent Areas, Interests, Strengths	Challenges	Interventions That Might Work to Differentiate
Robin	• Math and science • Animals • Great problem-solving skills	• Dyslexia diagnosis • Trouble with spelling, writing, and note-taking	• Use more complex mathematical problems/ processes without penalizing for spelling or writing errors. • Allow Robin to write math problems about animals for use in future assignments.
Matthew	• Music • Vivid imagination • Critical thinking skills • Strong reasoning ability	• Trouble focusing and remaining on-task for long periods of time • Impulsivity	• Have Matthew write songs to teach others about the topic being learned. • Break assignments down into smaller parts that require deeper thinking for shorter periods of time. • Challenge Matthew to create the shortest poem possible that still includes all vital parts of the lesson/unit.

on real-world application and abilities will motivate 2e students to show what they know about the material taught. Additionally, students should investigate authentic problems. By thinking and acting like professionals, students find the learning more relevant (Renzulli & Reis, 2014). Students can work collaboratively, giving themselves and each other feedback to improve. These types of active and authentic

Table 3
Interventions to Develop Executive Functioning Skills

Executive Functioning Skill	Interventions That May Help
Time management	• Plan how long each task/assignment will take with intermittent checkpoints at specified times. • Help student prioritize tasks to be completed. • Use smartphone apps as digital sticky notes for reminders.
Organization	• Provide graphic organizers, classroom routines, daily planner/calendar checked at school and home, or labeled notebook for each subject with sections for each type of paperwork kept (e.g., notes, homework, tests). • Help student store class items (e.g., pencils, papers) in consistent way in desk or notebook.
Self-monitoring	• Provide checklist at desk for self-monitoring. • Compare student's performance against standards set by teacher and student together before task begins.
Flexible thinking	• Visualize and discuss jokes, puns, and words with multiple meanings. • Look for alternative approaches to solving math problems. • Try studying differently for a quiz or test. • Use graphic organizers to organize ideas from a book or story.

learning opportunities allow 2e students to acquire new knowledge and skills in a more natural setting (Baum et al., 2017). Executive functioning skills, like time management and organization, should also be taught with strategies like backward planning, keeping a calendar, and creating to-do lists. More intervention ideas can be found in Table 3.

How Can Counselors Support Twice-Exceptional Learners?

Counselors should always consider the context before making recommendations to parents or teachers: Did a particular situation influence the child's behavior, and could it be avoided in future? Could a simple solution, like a new seating arrangement or schedule change, help? Counselors can identify antecedents that might have precipitated the child's escalation or negative behaviors, and then experiment with changing the environment in the classroom. Each student is unique, so various modifications may be attempted before finding something that works for each child. Often small concessions or variations will help the student maximize class time to learn. Sometimes learning about stress management and conflict resolution is helpful to 2e students (Baum et al., 2017).

Accommodations are important in AP and honors classes, too. These modifications often require either an Individualized Education Program (IEP) or a 504 plan created by the school. An IEP carries a special education label, while a 504 plan may be more flexible and easier to put in place. Although these plans usually focus on a child's weakness, they can instead focus on helping the child reach his or her academic potential. For instance, teachers might stipulate in the 504 plan that time in the gifted class cannot be withheld because of work not being turned in, or they might include enrichment opportunities to be given during the school day. Each child has unique needs and requires his or her own set of supports. Teachers can work with parents and the counselor to put modifications in place that will help students succeed in school.

Programming for 2e students may require flexibility on the school's part. Necessary components for each child's plan should include: attention to the child's strengths/developing talents, a challenging curriculum, both differentiated instruction and strategies that help the child accommodate areas of weakness, social-emotional support, and targeted remediation when required (Baum et al., 2017). Students' learning needs must be met in their area of talent with support and scaffolding to compensate for the disability. Counselors should gather data from many places (e.g., teachers, parents, doctors) to form an accurate picture of the social-emotional difficulties a student is experiencing. Just because a student does not report issues in an area, does not mean they do not exist (Foley-Nicpon & Assouline, 2015).

Counselors can also help these students prepare for college and future careers by considering both the talent domain and any area of disability when making recommendations. They can help students explore college options and careers that students may enjoy. Then, they can help students problem solve potential issues that might arise and determine a best-fit plan for students' future (Foley-Nicpon & Assouline, 2015).

Twice-exceptional students need to be resilient and have perseverance. Summer camps and enrichment experiences in areas of passion are particularly important for these students (Foley-Nicpon, 2018). Gifted students must be exposed to programs and activities that increase self-efficacy in their talent domain. For instance, a mathematically talented student could attend a summer enrichment camp at the Center for Talent Development at Northwestern University. Or, during the school year, the child might participate on the school's math club or robotics team. Experiences and camp are available for almost every talent domain area. Counselors can help point parents toward these resources.

Services should never be denied to 2e students; gifted coursework is a right, not a privilege. Teachers can consider a team approach rather than focusing on one data point or one composite score. In this way, educators can establish a more comprehensive view of the student using both qualitative and quantitative data. Foley-Nicpon, Assouline, and Fosenburg (2015) examined the relationship between self-concept and academic ability in 2e youth. They found that the overall self-concept of these students ($n = 64$) was in the average range. This might mean that their high cognitive ability served as a protective measure against negative feelings about their disabilities. Of the students in the study, most (about 70%) were receiving some sort of gifted academic programming. Withholding gifted services from 2e students can be considered discriminatory (Reis et al., 2014) and could possibly make their talent development pathway more difficult in school.

Reflection Questions

- What do you currently know that could encourage the talent development of 2e students? What can you do to improve your practice in this area?
- Have you taught or encountered students who have difficulties with executive functioning? How could you support their learning?
- In what ways could you involve the school counselor or psychologist to support your 2e students?

Opportunities to Practice

- What suggestions could you give parents who want to help their 2e children flourish?
- Develop a checklist that will help students monitor their time management or organization.

CHAPTER 5

Grouping and Acceleration Options for Gifted Students

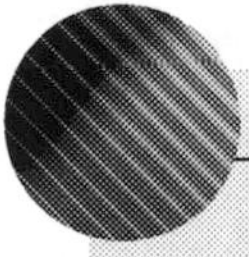

DRIVING QUESTION

How do educators create an environment that promotes advanced learning?

LEARNING TARGETS

- How should gifted learners be grouped for instruction?
- What is the research on acceleration and its effectiveness with gifted learners?
- Do Advanced Placement courses and International Baccalaureate programs meet the needs of gifted learners?

Grouping Gifted Learners

Homogeneous versus heterogeneous grouping has long been a controversial topic in education. Cross, Andersen, and Mammadov

DOI: 10.4324/9781003235330-6

(2015) pointed out that some researchers advocate for heterogeneous grouping. However, results of many studies in the field of gifted education show that gifted students benefit both academically and socio-emotionally from different forms of homogeneous grouping (Cross et al., 2015; Steenbergen-Hu, Makel, & Olszewski-Kubilius, 2016).

Ability Grouping

Ability grouping is defined as "any arrangement that attempts to place students with similar levels of ability in instructional groups" (Neihart, 2007, p. 333), enabling teachers to modify pace, instruction, and curriculum. Gifted students have specific learning needs that require a challenging curriculum and more exposure to students of similar ability. Grouping gifted learners by ability allows them to work at a pace that often exceeds the school's typical curriculum (Cross et al., 2015).

Steenbergen-Hu et al. (2016) categorized ability grouping into four main types:

- Between-class ability grouping—assigning students in the same grade into high, average, or low classes based on their prior achievement or ability levels.
- Within-class ability grouping—assigning students within a class to several small homogeneous groups for instruction based on students' prior achievement or learning capacities.
- Cross-grade subject grouping—grouping students of different grade levels together to learn a particular subject based on their prior achievement or learning potential.
- Special grouping for the gifted—designing programs specifically for gifted students, such as pull-out or honors programs. (p. 851)

Findings from this meta-analysis of 13 studies on ability groups (Steenbergen-Hu et al., 2016) showed that high-, average-, and low-ability students benefited, at least to a small degree, from within-class and cross-grade subject ability grouping. Benefits were negligible for between-class ability grouping. Gifted students benefited the most from being grouped in programs that were designed especially for them.

Results of a study by Vogl and Preckel (2014) supported the positive effects of students attending gifted classes. Students in these classes exhibited a positive social self-concept of acceptance, interest in school, and constructive student-teacher relationships.

Cluster Grouping

Cluster grouping, or Total School Cluster Grouping (TSCG), is a frequently used strategy for meeting the needs of gifted learners in the regular elementary classroom. This type of within-class grouping places 6–8 students identified as gifted, high achieving, or high ability into classrooms that consist of students of other achievement levels (Gentry, 2014; Steenbergen-Hu et al., 2016). Teachers in these classrooms must have an interest in working with gifted students and be willing to differentiate curriculum to meet their learning needs. Because cluster grouping places the highest achieving students in one classroom, it affects the composition of all of the other classrooms. Therefore, Gentry (2014) suggested using a TSCG approach, which considers the placement of *every* child in the school. Through achievement test results and student classroom performance, all students are identified as either high achieving, above-average achieving, average achieving, low-average achieving, or low achieving.

In addition to better meeting the needs of gifted learners, TSCG increases the likelihood that teachers will be able to meet the individual academic needs of all students, as the range of achievement levels in classrooms has been reduced. If a school adopts TSCG, the teachers and administrators must agree to the following (Gentry, 2014):

- Identification must occur yearly, with the expectation that all students will achieve and grow so that student placements might change from year to year.
- All student achievement levels are identified.
- The classrooms that contain the highest achieving students do not contain the lowest achieving students, as they are clustered in another classroom.

- In classrooms with students with special needs, teachers are provided with assistance.
- Teachers may flexibly group students between classrooms or among grade levels and flexibly group within their classrooms.
- All teachers receive professional development in gifted education strategies.
- The teacher who has the highest achieving students is selected by his or her colleagues and must differentiate instruction for these gifted learners.

Gentry also suggested that 2e students be placed in the high-achieving cluster so that the students' strengths become the educational focus.

Cluster grouping is often recommended as a research-based, cost-effective strategy to academically challenge gifted learners and to group them with peers. Research shows that groups of gifted students more often interact with intellectual peers and are provided with differentiated instruction when they are placed with a teacher who is trained to differentiate rather than when they are distributed among many teachers (Gentry, 2014). Additional research is needed, especially on the effects of academic and social-emotional needs of gifted learners in a cluster grouping environment. Gentry and her colleagues at Purdue University are currently involved in ongoing evaluation and longitudinal research on this model.

Pull-Out Programming

In a study on affective aspects of programs for gifted learners, Hornstra, van der Veen, and Peetsma (2017) described full-time and part-time high-ability programs. Because it is often difficult to meet the needs of gifted learners in regular classroom settings, many school districts create specialized programs for these students. Full-time programs are offered every day, all day. Part-time programs, also known as pull-out programs, are offered for only a few hours or a whole day each week in a setting outside of the students' regular classroom, and students attend their regular classroom during the rest of the week. The regular grade-level curriculum is usually accelerated in full-time programs so there is also time to offer enrichment opportunities for gifted learners. Part-time programs mainly focus on enrichment, often not related to the curriculum in the students' regular school, and might include project-based learning units that emphasize creative thinking, real-life problem solving, communication skills, critical thinking skills, and collaboration. Most often, full-time and part-time programs are offered at the elementary and middle school levels.

Hornstra et al. (2017) also expressed the advantage of both full- and part-time specialized programs: a more flexible curriculum that is tailored to meet the needs of gifted students and gives them the opportunity to interact with other high-ability learners.

Acceleration

Acceleration opportunities allow gifted learners to meet their individual educational goals at a more rapid pace. Empirical research indicates that acceleration has extremely positive effects on the academic and affective lives of gifted students (Gross, 2006; Rogers, 2015). Despite these encouraging findings, many gifted learners are not provided with acceleration opportunities to better meet their individual needs (Callahan, Moon, & Oh, 2014).

Acceleration options fall into two main categories: subject-based acceleration and grade-based acceleration (Assouline, Colangelo, VanTassel-Baska, & Lupkowski-Shoplik, 2015; Rogers, 2015). When using subject-based acceleration, gifted students learn advanced content and skills in areas of special talent or interest to them at an earlier age than their peers. Grade-based acceleration involves shortening the number of years that gifted learners remain in the K–12 system before enrolling in college. Because acceleration can be achieved by using materials and courses that school districts already have in place, the cost involved is minimal (Assouline et al., 2015).

Although there are many different ways to provide acceleration for students, many of these options are underutilized by teachers and administrators. In a survey study by Callahan et al. (2014), 1,566 school districts from across the country answered questions about the use of acceleration options. Of the responding districts, less that 2.5%

of elementary and middle schools offered subject or whole-grade acceleration. High school acceleration opportunities were most often provided through Advanced Placement, International Baccalaureate, and dual enrollment courses. By using many available acceleration options, educators can tailor acceleration decisions to benefit individual gifted students.

Grade-skipping, one form of acceleration, offers many benefits for gifted students. Grade-skipping can happen at any time during the academic journey—from early entrance to kindergarten to early college admission. The effects of grade-skipping are positive and larger than for most other acceleration strategies (Steenbergen-Hu & Moon, 2011). Gross (2006) compared students who were accelerated to those who were not accelerated. Her findings indicated that early elementary students who were accelerated 2 or more years had far greater social self-esteem in childhood and better social relations later in life.

Either due to misinformation or lack of information, many educators do not recommend or support grade-based acceleration. Some cite concerns for students' social and emotional development. Others report that they fear their recommendation could be met by resistance from administrators, parents, or other educators (Siegle, Wilson, & Little, 2013). Rambo and McCoach (2012) found that teachers acknowledged the positive effects of acceleration but still put more weight on the possible negative effects.

Because the decision to accelerate a student is sometimes difficult and controversial, the Iowa Acceleration Scale was developed to guide educators and determine if grade-skipping is an appropriate option for a particular student (Assouline, Colangelo, Lupkowski-Shoplik, Lipscomb, & Forstadt, 2009). This scale provides a systematic and objective decision-making structure to help educators and parents make recommendations for grade-skipping with confidence. Among the factors considered are the student's academic ability, aptitude, and achievement; school and academic factors; developmental factors; interpersonal skills; and attitude and support. Each factor is given a numeric value, which helps to guide the discussion, decision making, and planning for acceleration.

Advanced Placement and International Baccalaureate Programs

The Advanced Placement program, created by the College Board, offers academically prepared students the opportunity to pursue more rigorous college-level studies while still in high school. AP courses are modeled on comparable introductory college courses in several subject categories in as many as 38 courses (College Board, 2019). Within each AP course, a culminating end-of-course exam is given and scored on a scale of 1 to 5 by university professors and experienced AP teachers. If students score a 3 or higher on this exam, many universities give students credit or allow them to exempt out of introductory courses.

Schools offering International Baccalaureate (IB) programs must be certified by the International Baccalaureate Organization (IBO, 2019). Schools can become IB schools if they meet the rigorous and extensive requirements established by the IBO. The International Baccalaureate program most commonly offered throughout the United States is the IB Diploma (IBD) program for high school students ages 16–19. The IBD program emphasizes an internationally standardized curriculum made up of six subject groups and the IBD core, comprised of theory of knowledge, creativity, activity, and service, as well as an extended essay. IBD courses also end with a culminating exam. Colleges and universities differ in their approaches to offering credit for IB exams.

Although AP and IB programs were not designed to specifically meet the needs of gifted students, they are the most prevalent ways in which an accelerated curriculum is offered for high school students. Hertberg-Davis and Callahan (2008) conducted a study of gifted students' perceptions of AP and IB programs. They reported that most gifted students were satisfied with the curriculum and instruction within AP and IB courses, and perceived these courses as challenging and among the "best" courses offered at their schools. The students interviewed especially appreciated being in classes with similarly motivated peers and with teachers who respected and understood them.

However, Hertberg-Davis and Callahan (2008) also reported that gifted students who dropped out of AP or IB courses said the way these courses were taught did not allow them to succeed, feel welcome, or learn in the ways they liked to learn. Hertberg-Davis and Callahan offered five recommendations for how gifted students' experiences in AP and IB courses could be enriched:

- Teachers should emphasize appreciation of these courses as a genuine challenge and meaningful learning rather than emphasizing high exam scores.
- AP and IB teachers should receive consistent training to teach these courses. Present inconsistencies result in teachers offering varying levels of challenge, having uneven content knowledge, and using inappropriate methods.
- Equity within AP and IB courses should be a priority, enabling all talented learners to succeed, regardless of background experiences, culture, ethnicity, or socioeconomic status.
- AP and IB teachers need professional development to learn how to differentiate instruction for a broad range of gifted learners. Most teachers who participated in the study had little or no training in gifted education.
- High schools can also offer other course options, such as mentorships, internships, and externships; accelerated pre-AP and IB options; independent studies; enrichment opportunities; dual enrollment; and weekly special interest seminars.

Reflection Questions

- How can homogeneous grouping benefit advanced learners in a school/district? What barriers prevent this type of grouping, and how can they be overcome?
- What is happening in the schools/districts around you regarding issues of accelerated learning? Have you encountered any compelling research or stories on the different sides of the issue?
- What questions would you like to ask educators, parents, or other stakeholders about the risks and benefits of acceleration?

Opportunities for Practice

- Investigate AP or IB programs in a local school district. Interview students to determine their satisfaction with the curriculum and instruction in these programs. Are students being academically challenged? How are they being taught to succeed? How is instruction in these classes helping them learn in the ways they like to learn?
- Develop a grouping strategy for a particular subject or class that will allow you to either accelerate or enrich content for your highest learners. Explain what data you will use to group students and be specific about how you will challenge them.

CHAPTER 6

Differentiating Curriculum, Assessment, and Instruction for Gifted Learners

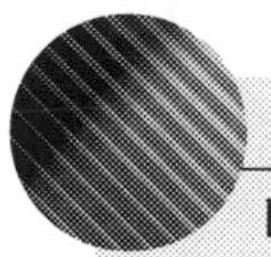

DRIVING QUESTION

How can educators help gifted learners maximize their school performance?

LEARNING TARGETS

- How can curriculum content and assessment be modified to meet the needs of gifted learners?
- How does differentiating instruction enhance learning for gifted learners?
- What teaching strategies and curriculum modifications support gifted learners' needs?

Modifying Curriculum Content and Assessment

All students are entitled to an effective curriculum that is differentiated to meet individual needs. Good curriculum and instruction for

DOI: 10.4324/9781003235330-7

gifted learners begin with good curriculum and instruction for all—curriculum that is meaning-making, rich, and high level (Tomlinson, 2005). VanTassel-Baska and Hubbard (2016) stated that gifted students need to be exposed to content at their level of functioning and beyond. If they master the material within a particular unit, they need to be provided with more advanced content and learning activities, not more of the same material. As students are studying advanced content accompanied by meaningful learning activities, they should be provided with complex and challenging subject-matter resources. Teachers can provide gifted students the opportunity to use cutting-edge supplemental texts and technological resources, such as eBooks, podcasts, blogs, social networks, discussion forums, online journals, and online magazines and newspapers (Hébert & Pagnani, 2010). Gifted educators and students can also make use of technology with "games, videos, simulations, interactive activities, virtual reality environments, real-time data, calculators, data analysis tools, and text of every kind" (Housand, Housand, & Renzulli, 2017, p. 157). Technology can be a helpful tool for differentiating instruction for gifted learners.

Gifted students should also interact with mentors who have specialized knowledge and skills in a common area of interest. Through various technology tools, access to mentors can be greatly increased no matter what subject area, level of expertise, or geographical constraint. E-mail, text messaging, webcams, blogs, and wikis make communication with mentors fast and easy (Zimlich, 2017). Through technology, mentors can provide opportunities for students to function as research aides (for scientists, mathematicians, historians, etc.) and allow them to understand what experts do in their fields. Housand et al. (2017) suggested using Skype, Google Hangouts, and FaceTime to connect with mentors. Teachers can also join Nepris (https://www.nepris.com), an organization that connects students with an expert in industry.

The curriculum at any grade level is usually dictated by standards, curriculum guides, and textbooks (Tomlinson, 2005). Local or state standards may not be adequate, rigorous, or rich enough for gifted students. Gifted learners need fewer repetitions to learn new content and can grasp more advanced concepts earlier (Stambaugh, 2014); therefore, they will need to study content standards with more depth and complexity. Educators will need to know the vertical alignment of content area standards in order to tap into standards within the same strand of higher grade levels and then accelerate learning when necessary.

Preassessment and Ongoing Assessment

NAGC (2010) developed the Pre-K to Grade 12 Gifted Programming Standards. Standard 2 addresses forms of assessment practices essential for gifted students. Specifically, Standard 2.4.1 states that "educators use differentiated pre- and post- performance-based assessments to measure the progress of students with gifts and talents."

The pace of instructional delivery should be consistent with individual students' progress (NAGC, 2010). Preassessment and ongoing assessment can help educators adjust instruction, leading to a positive educational experience for gifted learners. Preassessments establish the baseline for growth and the instructional level needed. By assessing students' current level of knowledge and skill, educators can ensure that new learning will take place as a result of instruction. When preassessments are omitted, instruction often focuses on content the students already know. Results from preassessments help determine what extension, enrichment, or acceleration options might be appropriate.

Preassessment tools. Tools and data that could be used for preassessment purposes are readily available to educators, including mandatory standardized state and district achievement tests. Achievement tests are used to determine what students have learned and can help teachers determine which students are more advanced than their grade-level peers. Common achievement tests include the Terra Nova/CTBS, Iowa Test of Basic Skills (ITBS), California Achievement Test (CAT), Stanford Achievement Test (SAT), and Measure of Academic Progress (MAP). The best types of standardized achievement tests have no ceiling, allowing students to show all of what they know. Caution should be taken when using information from these tests with ELLs, students with learning disabilities, or those from low-income or minority backgrounds. These underserved learners are often excluded from services for gifted learners if standardized test results are the only tools used (NAGC, n.d.).

School districts develop curriculum and purchase texts that contain end-of-chapter tests. Often, there are two versions of these—both paper/pencil and digital formats. These tests can also be used for preassessment purposes if given before teaching a chapter or unit.

Voluntary preassessment. After some direct instruction on a new topic, teachers can offer students a chance to take the end-of-chapter test. Students can be told that if they score a certain percentage on this test, they will not have to do the regular assignments for this topic and can work on more advanced extension activities instead. Some students will accept this offer, whereas others will decide that they need the practice work for the chapter or unit.

At times, teachers will develop their own preassessments. Many of the most effective types of preassessments are informal (see Online Resources for examples of informal preassessments). Preassessing should not be a lengthy process and should simply address what students should know and be able to do by the end of a lesson or unit.

Interest inventories. Interest inventories provide information about what gifted students need to make their learning more relevant. Interest inventories can be created to survey general interests or can focus on specific topics. In addition to students' personal interests, concerns, fads/trends, talents, and future careers, general interest inventories might survey students' thinking style preferences (i.e., analytic, creative, practical and/or auditory, visual, linguistic, kinesthetic); learning environment preferences (i.e., work alone, with a partner, in small groups, with an adult); instructional style preferences (i.e., lecture, project-based, Socratic seminars); and product preferences (i.e., written, oral, multimedia, artistic, performance). Specific topic inventories delve further into students' interests and preferences regarding details related to an upcoming unit. Renzulli and Reis (2014) developed a student-friendly interest inventory called the *Interest-A-Lyzer*. The information learned from preassessments and interest inventories can benefit the achievement of gifted students.

Formative assessment. Formative assessment must continually be used to adjust the pace and to enrich and/or accelerate the curriculum for gifted students. Formative assessments can be administered formally or informally.

Performance-based assessments. Well-designed, performance-based final assessments can help educators evaluate a student's level of knowledge and skill acquisition, higher level reasoning abilities, and product development (Chappuis, Stiggins, Chappuis, & Arter, 2012). When designing a performance task for gifted learners, VanTassel-Baska (2014b) recommended that the task be challenging and open-ended to encourage creativity. Performance assessments provide gifted students the chance to demonstrate complex thinking about meaningful content, to make connections across disciplines, and to apply learning to real-world scenarios (Moon & Callahan, 2000). Performance-based assessments align well with project-based learning (VanTassel-Baska, 2014b) and often call for students to develop a product, such as a research paper, scientific experiment, or presentation, to demonstrate their knowledge or skills. When asking students to develop these types of products, teachers should present a scenario or situation that simulates what professionals would do in a real-world context (Moon & Callahan, 2000). Also, teachers should include well-written rubrics so students understand the expectations for the task. (An example of a performance-based assessment and rubric can be found in the Online Resources.)

Differentiating Instruction for Enhanced Learning

Differentiating instruction involves tailoring the content, process, product, and/or learning environment to better meet individual students' readiness levels, interests, and learning profiles (Tomlinson & Imbeau, 2010). Gifted learners usually make connections within and among disciplines, learn at a quicker pace and with more depth than their peers, and have a variety of interests. These characteristics could be evident in all subject areas or in specific subjects. Gifted learners must be able to stretch and grow daily in a school setting. Therefore, teachers need to be familiar with strategies that can be used to differentiate instruction for these students.

In a position paper on differentiation of curriculum and instruction, NAGC (2014) maintained that effective differentiation for gifted students not only makes use of acceleration, but also ensures that there are open-ended opportunities to meet the standards through multiple pathways, more complex thinking applications, and real-world problem-solving contexts.

Teaching Strategies and Curricular Modifications

According to Reis, Westberg, Kulikowich, and Purcell (1998), "curriculum can be modified to better meet the needs of high ability students through strategies that differentiate the curriculum: higher level questioning skills, curriculum compacting, independent study, tiered assignments, flexible grouping and the use of advanced content" (p. 123). The following sections explore these strategies. Examples of many of the models can be found in the Online Resources.

Higher Level Questioning Skills

In any curriculum, questions tend to guide the level of thought expected of students (VanTassel-Baska & Hubbard, 2016). Teachers must model critical and creative thinking by asking questions that require students to think more meaningfully and divergently about content. Using deliberate questions is an important strategy for getting gifted students to think in more complex and in-depth ways (VanTassel-Baska, 2014a). In a qualitative case study, Sak (2004) found that teacher beliefs and practices were key in improving students' critical and creative thinking. Students must be provided with experiences and tools that encourage them to generate their own higher level questions so they can develop innovative ideas, solutions, and products. According to Sternberg and Spear-Swerling (2002), "Learning how to ask questions plays as important a role in the development of thinking as does learning how to answer questions" (p. 149). Questions can be improved by using models for construction (VanTassel-Baska, 2014a). By frequently engaging with a variety of critical and creative thinking strategies applied to appropriate curriculum, gifted learners will also be better prepared to explore questions posed to them (Hickerson, 2013).

Critical Thinking Skills Models

Bloom's taxonomy. Bloom's (1956) taxonomy is the most common framework used to encourage higher order thinking skills. The revised version (Anderson & Krathwohl, 2001) updated the thinking skills hierarchy from knowledge, comprehension, application, analysis, synthesis, and evaluation, to remember, understand, apply, analyze, evaluate, and create. This shift reminds educators that *creating* new knowledge is the most demanding cognitive process. Note that Anderson and Krathwohl did not take knowledge out of the cognitive processes, but instead added it as a separate dimension with four different types:

- **Factual knowledge:** Knowledge of terminology and specific details.
- **Conceptual knowledge:** Knowledge of categories, generalizations, and theories.
- **Procedural knowledge:** Knowledge of subject-specific skills, algorithms, techniques, and methods.
- **Metacognitive knowledge:** Knowledge about cognitive tasks and self-knowledge.

Gifted learners often rapidly acquire the knowledge base needed within a discipline, so they should spend the majority of their time working at the higher levels of Bloom's taxonomy. According to Hickerson (2013),

> Gifted students need to be involved with analysis, evaluation, and creative synthesis of data and information, asking new questions and generating innovative ideas, solutions, and products because of their advanced cognitive development, preference for complexity, questioning of the status quo, idealism, and need for social action. (p. 15)

Bloom's taxonomy can be taught to gifted learners to help them understand what is involved in each level, especially the levels of higher order thinking. Both teachers and students can use questions framed from the taxonomy as discussion starters, for independent study tasks, for developing tiered assignments, as extension activity ideas, and for assessments (see Online Resources for examples).

Paul Model of Reasoning. Paul and Elder (2006) stated that excellent critical thinkers ask important questions about issues and problems. The Paul Model of Reasoning can be used by teachers to structure questions in purposeful ways to stimulate higher level thinking or to help gifted learners ask relevant questions about various aspects of a current issue (VanTassel-Baska, 2014a). The Paul Model has eight elements that guide critical questioning (see Online Resources).

Depth and complexity. Kaplan and Gould (1998) extensively researched what distinguishes experts' knowledge in a field of study compared to those with only surface knowledge. They categorized expert knowledge in two ways:

- **Depth:** Encourages students to look further, deeper, and with greater elaboration into the content in a field of study.
- **Complexity:** Helps students make connections and identify relationships between, within, and across different subjects and disciplines.

Further, Kaplan and Gould (1998) developed eight tools/prompts to help students understand what is involved in mastering a topic or field with depth, and three tools/prompts pertaining to complexity (see Online Resources for examples). Icons were designed to help students remember and use each of the depth and complexity tools.

Creative Thinking Skills Models

Fostering student creativity has become an added responsibility for classroom teachers. It could be argued there is limited time to develop students' creative potential in a system with high-stakes testing requirements that focus on convergent thinking. However, in this 21st-century world in which a nation's economic growth is increasingly innovation-driven, creativity has become a desired learning goal (Tan, Lee, Ponnusamy, Koh, & Tan, 2016).

Traditionally, creativity was thought to be found mostly within the subjects of music, art, literature, and dance. However, creativity should permeate all subjects (Soh, 2017). Blamires and Peterson

(2014) argued that because creativity requires knowledge and skills to provide a purpose, creativity should be taught and used within subject disciplines. Therefore, all teachers need to know more about creative thinking and the best ways to teach for creative growth, as well as how to use important strategies such as creative problem solving (Tan et al., 2016). Soh (2017) asserted that teaching behaviors play a critical role in cultivating student creativity. One way students learn to be creative is by imitating the behavior of their teachers.

Everyone has tremendous creative potential. Creative skills can be learned and enhanced. Kettler, Lamb, and Mullet (2018) summarized the work of Torrance, who, in 1972, investigated if students could be taught to think creatively. As Torrance reviewed more than 130 studies, he found that "deliberate teaching made the biggest difference in teaching students to think creatively" (as cited in Kettler et al., 2018, p. 81). The creative thinking strategies presented here can help educators use creative behaviors that will teach students to generate numerous, varied, and innovative possibilities, and then choose effective solutions for problem situations.

Williams Model. Williams (1993) developed the Cognitive-Affective Interaction Model. One dimension within the Williams Model consists of eight processes deduced from several theoretical studies of how people think divergently. The first four levels (fluency, flexibility, originality, and elaboration) are cognitive domains, and the last four (risk-taking, complexity, curiosity, and imagination) are affective domains. The four affective factors come from studies of the dispositions of highly creative people. These eight processes are an extension of Anderson and Krathwohl's (2001) *create* level of thinking. Williams contended that all eight processes need to be addressed in the classroom (see Online Resources for examples).

SCAMPER. SCAMPER is a very helpful divergent thinking tool used to spur fluency and flexibility. SCAMPER is a mnemonic that helps the user ask questions about an existing product or idea in order to generate creative ideas to develop something new. Osborn (1963) developed many of the questions used in this strategy; however, Eberle (2008) organized these questions into SCAMPER (substitute, combine, adapt, modify/magnify/minify, put to other uses, eliminate, and reverse/rearrange). This tool can be used to assist students when brainstorming novel ideas for writing a creative story, dreaming up innovative ideas in a Makerspace environment, using the engineering design process to improve a product, or solving an ill-structured problem (see Online Resources for an example). A study by Hussain and Carignan (2016) explored to what extent the SCAMPER tool helped fourth-grade students create novel ideas during an animal adaptation science unit. The final product made by students using SCAMPER charts to assist with brainstorming showed more complexity and originality.

Creative problem solving. The creative problem solving (CPS) model has had several iterations since its inception in the 1950s by Osborn and Parnes, and continues to evolve today. The most familiar model, called the Osborn-Parnes Five Stage CPS Model, includes the stages of Fact Finding, Problem Finding, Idea Finding, Solution Finding, and Acceptance Finding (Creative Education Foundation, 2015). The most recent CPS Model developed by the Creative Education Foundation (2015) has four stages: clarify, ideate, develop, and implement. Creative problem solving involves both divergent thinking (generating many different ideas) and convergent thinking (evaluating and bringing together different ideas to make decisions). See Online Resources for a unit example.

Six hats thinking. De Bono (1999) developed a tool to stimulate group discussion and individual thinking that uses a metaphor of six different hat colors, encouraging participants to focus on one type of thinking at a time—called parallel thinking. By using and changing hat colors, group members can challenge themselves to think clearly and thoroughly in different directions. When groups use the six hats thinking process, they tend to act more collaboratively. When the hats are used by an individual person, they help the user address a problem from a variety of angles. Both critical and creative thinking are used in this process. Teachers can use the hats to discuss how the academic needs of gifted learners are being served in most school districts (see Online Resources).

Process Strategies

Teachers can use the information from each of the preceding models and tools to develop the following process strategies to differentiate instruction for gifted learners.

Curriculum Compacting

Curriculum compacting is a differentiated instructional technique that targets students who have already mastered the information the rest of the class needs to learn, allowing these students to accelerate their learning or to participate in enrichment or extension options. Many gifted students become bored or frustrated because they are held accountable for information they already know (Reis & Renzulli, 1995). Reis et al. (1998) reported findings from a study in which teachers offered curriculum compacting to a targeted group of gifted students. When teachers eliminated as much as 50% of regular curricular activities for these students, no differences were observed in posttest achievement scores between treatment and control groups. Although the gifted students spent much less time on the standards, they were able to master just as much of the content.

Curriculum compacting can be used in any subject area at any grade level. Most literature on curriculum compacting suggests three steps to this process:

1. Define the goals or outcomes of a unit of study.
2. Determine and document which students have mastered all or most of these goals.
3. Provide replacement options that are more challenging and make productive use of these students' time.

Renzulli and Smith (1979) developed "The Compactor," a management form for guiding the curriculum compacting process. One form should be completed for each student who is participating in compacting and should be shared with the student and his or her parents/guardians. The form should be updated regularly and kept in the student's academic files.

Interest-Based Independent Study

Interest-based independent study is a differentiated technique that can foster high motivation for achievement in gifted students. Students develop critical and creative thinking skills, delve deeply into issues for topics of special interest, and develop self-reliance and resourcefulness skills as they design and then carry out their own learning in a flexible and comfortable environment (Powers, 2008; Westberg & Leppien, 2018). When gifted learners are interested in a topic, studying that topic can hold their attention for long periods of time. Powers (2008) examined motivation factors for academic achievement among gifted learners. Students involved in independent study noted that the opportunity was educational, interesting, fun, and informative.

Educators can connect students' interests to academic performance by allowing students to have voice and choice. As students implement an independent study plan, teachers take on a supportive role and become a resource for students. Independent studies work especially well for gifted learners who are self-directed. Educators should use caution with students who lack self-discipline or those who procrastinate. These students will need to have frequent teacher-student conferences and a structured plan that includes specific deadlines. Direct instruction or small-group instruction will need to be provided as students are working on various aspects of independent work.

Students should be asked to develop and answer a meaningful question through research, use a variety of resources, and effectively communicate their findings. Teachers will need to plan how to develop, monitor, and assess learning as students carry out an investigation. Powers (2008) developed a field-tested, research-based plan for what should be included in an independent study. The recommended time period for an independent study using the Powers plan is 2 weeks. See Online Resources for an overview of the six-part plan.

Other researchers have developed models and given suggestions for independent study. VanTassel-Baska and Little (2017) emphasized that in addition to helping students study a topic that they really care about, teachers can help students do an independent study about a real-world issue involving their topic. This will encourage authentic learning and will make the research project more student-centered and inquiry-based. Westberg and Leppien (2018) advised that teachers should decide whether they give students the flexibility to develop independent studies on any topic of interest or on topics within specific disciplines. No matter the decision, the following suggestions are offered:

- Have students complete an interest inventory to help them focus on a few areas of interest or brainstorm.
- Help students formulate a number of "I wonder . . ." questions about their topic.
- Provide students with possible authentic product ideas (see Online Resources).
- Help students find an appropriate authentic audience to present the results of their independent investigations.

Westberg and Leppien (2018) additionally suggested that if students are expected to conduct investigations like professionals, teachers need to provide instruction so students can develop research skills, such as formulating hypotheses, conducting interviews and observations, summarizing and depicting data, managing time, documenting sources, and detecting bias.

Tiered Assignments

Tiered assignments are another differentiated strategy that allows students of different readiness levels to work with the same knowledge and skills (Tomlinson, 2014). Instead of using a one-size-fits-all approach, tiering allows for different readiness level groups to use different levels of complexity, open-endedness, and independence as they complete an assignment. Tomlinson suggested the following steps to tier an assignment:

1. Identify the standard(s) to focus on as the tiered assignment is developed. Clearly determine what all students need to know, understand, and/or be able to do.
2. Think about the data gained from formative assessments, as well as students' learning strengths and interests.
3. Develop one assignment that is interesting, engaging, and clearly focused on the learning goals (for the needs of the

most advanced learners). Then create various scaffolded versions to support the needs of other learners.

4. Depending on the version of the assignment, vary the materials students use, develop a range of learning applications by thinking about the complexity of the task, and/or allow students to express their learning by offering a variety of products.
5. Match the most appropriate task to each student based on his or her readiness needs. The goal is to challenge all students and provide the support necessary for their success.
6. Note that tiering does not mean more/less or harder/easier work. It means *different* work that engages students to think critically.

An example of a tiered assignment can be found in the Online Resources.

Extension Activities and Choice

Extension activities are a type of enrichment strategy that allows students to work on a topic with more depth and breadth. Substantive extension activities may involve offering a choice of options about a specific topic from some kind of menu or choice board. Choice is important in fostering gifted behaviors, such as creativity or motivation (de Souza Fleith, 2000). Student engagement will also increase if students are given flexible directions for assignments and the opportunity to collaborate with others based on mutual interest. Students usually work on these learning activities independently, but the teacher offers support when necessary. There are many different types of choice boards or menus.

Tic-tac-toe choices. This type of choice menu is developed by using a traditional tic-tac-toe board, with nine (3 x 3) spaces. A challenging question or learning activity is placed within each space on the board, and students choose three activities by forming a row, column, or diagonal tic-tac-toe. When designing learning activities or challenging questions for a tic-tac-toe board, teachers can create options that include higher levels of Bloom's (1956) taxonomy or make use of Kaplan and Gould's (1998) depth and complexity tools. Teachers should give students explicit directions and clear deadlines (see Online Resources for examples).

RAFTS choices. Designed to encourage writing across the curriculum, RAFTS stands for:

- assume a Role (e.g., student, lawyer, engineer, teacher),
- carefully consider the Audience (e.g., school board, jury, planning commission),
- write in a particular Format (e.g., newspaper article, essay, play, video),
- research a relevant Topic, and
- consider a Strong verb or feeling.

As these options are developed, teachers can use roles, formats, and topics that appeal to a variety of interests. It is expected that students do a great deal of research on the topic before beginning to work on the product. Because gifted learners should work independently on this enrichment option, teachers can consider using task cards to further explain what is expected as students work on the final product for each choice. (See Online Resources for examples of RAFTS, choices, and task cards.) This enrichment activity could also be used as a replacement option when using curriculum compacting.

TriMind choices. Sternberg and Spear-Swerling's (2002) Triarchic Theory of Intelligence can be used to develop TriMind tasks. Sternberg categorized intelligences into three different areas:

- componential intelligence, which focuses on analytic skills (abstract thinking and logical reasoning, strong verbal skills);
- experiential intelligence, which features creativity (divergent thinking, ability to deal with novel situations); and
- contextual intelligence, which emphasizes practical intelligence (application of knowledge to the real world).

Again, students should be provided with choices that are centered around the *same* learning goal(s) as those of the rest of the class but are designed to tap into each of these intelligence strengths (see Online Resources for examples).

Project-Based Learning

Project-based learning (PBL) is a curriculum model that incorporates higher order thinking skills and 21st-century skills, such as critical thinking, creative thinking, innovation, authentic problem solving, collaboration, and communication. PBL is advocated by numerous scholars who agree that it motivates students and develops content area expertise and technology skills (Brinkley, 2018). PBLWorks (Larmer, 2015) developed an extensive "gold standard" model that contains Key Knowledge, Understanding, and Success Skills, as well as seven comprehensive and research-based essential design elements to help teachers develop PBL units. (See Online Resources for an explanation of how each of the design elements addresses the needs of gifted students.)

Reflection Questions

- As you think about developing a unit, is the content suitable for gifted learners? Why or why not? What supplemental resources will you provide?
- How has your thinking about using different types of assessments for gifted students changed? What will you do differently now?
- Why is PBL appropriate for gifted students? In a mixed-ability classroom, how would you group gifted students during a PBL unit?

Opportunities for Practice

- Plan a new unit with gifted learners in mind. Consider what resources you will need to advance the content for these students and how you will summatively assess the unit so that students will demonstrate creative and critical thinking.

- During a unit of study, what models and tools will you use to increase questioning strategies for gifted learners?
- Using the Online Resources examples for curriculum compacting, independent study, tiered assignments, and extension learning activities, design a plan using one of these strategies.
- Research and collect strategies and activities related to the ones mentioned in this chapter that would be appropriate for gifted learners.

References

Anderson, L., & Krathwohl, D. R. (Eds.). (2001). *A taxonomy for learning, teaching, and assessing: A revision of Bloom's taxonomy of educational objectives* (Complete ed.). New York, NY: Longman.

Assouline, S., Colangelo, N., Lupkowski-Shoplik, A., Lipscomb, J., & Forstadt, L. (2009). *Iowa Acceleration Scale manual: A guide for whole-grade acceleration K–8* (3rd ed.). Scottsdale, AZ: Great Potential Press.

Assouline, S., Colangelo, N., VanTassel-Baska, J., & Lupkowski-Shoplik, A. (Eds.). (2015). *A nation empowered: Evidence trumps the excuses that hold back America's brightest students* (Vol. 2). Iowa City: University of Iowa, The Connie Belin & Jacqueline N. Blank International Center for Gifted Education and Talent Development.

Baum, S. M., Renzulli, S., & Rizza, M. G. (2015). Twice-exceptional adolescents: Who are they? What do they need? In F. A. Dixon & S. M. Moon (Eds.), *The handbook of secondary gifted education* (2nd ed., pp. 155–184). Waco, TX: Prufrock Press.

Baum, S. M., Schader, R. M., & Owen, S. V. (2017). *To be gifted and learning disabled: Strength-based strategies for helping twice-exceptional students with LD, ADHD, ASD, and more* (3rd ed.). Waco, TX: Prufrock Press.

Beason-Manes, A. D. (2018). Community activism as curriculum: How to meet gifted students' needs while creating change. *Gifted Child Today, 41,* 19–27.

Beghetto, R. A., Kaufman, J. C., & Baer, J. (2015). *Teaching for creativity in the Common Core classroom*. New York, NY: Teachers College Press.

Blamires, M., & Peterson, A. (2014). Can creativity be assessed? Towards an evidence-informed framework for assessing and planning progress in creativity. *Cambridge Journal of Education, 44,* 147–162.

Bloom, B. (Ed.). (1956). *Taxonomy of educational objectives: The classification of educational goals. Handbook I: Cognitive domain.* New York, NY: Longmans Green.

Brinkley, T. (2018). Technology for gifted students in mixed-ability classrooms. In J. Cannaday (Ed.), *Curriculum development for gifted education programs* (pp. 100–134). Hershey, PA: IGI Global.

Bruce-Davis, M. N., & Chancey, J. M. (2012). Connecting students to the real world: Developing gifted behaviors through service learning. *Psychology in the Schools, 49,* 716–723.

Callahan, C. M., Moon, T. R., & Oh, S. (2014). *National surveys of gifted programs: Executive summary.* Charlottesville: University of Virginia, National Research Center on the Gifted and Talented.

Chappuis, J., Stiggins, R. J., Chappuis, S., & Arter, J. A. (2012). *Classroom assessment for student learning: Doing it right—using it well* (2nd ed.). Boston, MA: Pearson.

Coleman, L. J., & Cross, T. L. (2005). *Being gifted in school: An introduction to development, guidance, and teaching* (2nd ed.). Waco, TX: Prufrock Press.

College Board. (2019). *AP courses and exams.* Retrieved from https://apstudent.collegeboard.org/apcourse

Creative Education Foundation. (2015). *Creative problem solving resource guide.* Scituate, MA: Author.

Cross, J. R., Frazier, A. D., Kim, M., & Cross, T. L. (2018). A comparison of perceptions of barriers to academic success among high-ability students from high- and low-income groups: Exposing poverty of a different kind. *Gifted Child Quarterly, 62,* 111–129.

Cross, T. L. (2016). The role of contagion in suicidal behavior among students with gifts and talents. *Gifted Child Today, 39,* 63–66.

Cross, T. L., Andersen, L., & Mammadov, S. (2015). Effects of academic acceleration on the social and emotional lives of gifted students. In S. G. Assouline, N. Colangelo, J. VanTassel-Baska, & Lupkowski-Shoplik (Eds.), *A nation empowered: Evidence trumps the excuses holding back America's brightest students* (Vol. 2, pp. 31–42). Iowa City: University of Iowa, The Connie Belin & Jacqueline N. Blank International Center for Gifted Education and Talent Development.

de Bono, E. (1999). *Six thinking hats* (Revised and updated ed.). Boston, MA: Little, Brown.

de Souza Fleith, D. (2000). Teacher and student's perceptions of creativity in the classroom environment. *Roeper Review, 22,* 148–153.

Doss, K. K., & Bloom, L. (2018). Mindfulness in the middle school classroom: Strategies to target social and emotional well-being of gifted students. *Gifted Education International, 34,* 181–192.

Eberle, B. (2008). *Scamper: Creative games for imagination development* (Combined ed.). Waco, TX: Prufrock Press.

Eddles-Hirsch, K., Vialle, W., Rogers, K. B., & McCormick, J. (2010). "Just challenge those high-ability learners and they'll be all right!" The impact of social context and challenging instruction on the affective development of high-ability students. *Journal of Advanced Academics, 22,* 106–128.

Evans, E. A. (2015). *Young, gifted, Black, and blocked: A critical inquiry of barriers that hinder Black students' participation in gifted and advanced placement programs* (Doctoral dissertation). Retrieved from Electronic Theses & Dissertations. (1355)

Foley-Nicpon, M. (2018, November). *What works for twice-exceptional youth?* Session presented at the meeting of the National Association for Gifted Children Conference, Minneapolis, MN.

Foley-Nicpon, M., & Assouline, S. G. (2015). Counseling considerations for the twice-exceptional client. *Journal of Counseling & Development, 93,* 202–211.

Foley-Nicpon, M., Assouline, S. G., & Fosenburg, S. (2015). The relationship between self-concept, ability, and academic programming among twice-exceptional youth. *Journal of Advanced Academics, 26,* 256–273.

Foley-Nicpon, M., Assouline, S. G., Kivlighan, D. M., Fosenburg, S., Cederberg, C., & Nanji, M. (2017). The effects of a social and talent development intervention for high ability youth with social skill difficulties. *High Ability Studies, 28,* 73–92.

Ford, D. Y. (2010). Underrepresentation of culturally different students in gifted education: Reflections about current problems and recommendations for the future. *Gifted Child Today, 33*(3), 31.

Freeman, J. (2006). Giftedness in the long term. *Journal for the Education of the Gifted, 29,* 384–403.

Gaesser, A. H. (2018). Befriending anxiety to reach potential: Strategies to empower our gifted youth. *Gifted Child Today, 41,* 186–195.

Gagné, F. (2015). Academic talent development programs: A best practices model. *Asia Pacific Education Review, 16,* 281–295.

Gentry, M. (2014). *Total school cluster grouping and differentiation: A comprehensive research-based plan for raising student achievement and improving teacher practices* (2nd ed.). Waco, TX: Prufrock Press.

Gotlieb, R., Hyde, E., Immordino-Yang, M. H., & Kaufman, S. B. (2016). Cultivating the social-emotional imagination in gifted education: Insights from educational neuroscience. *Annals of the New York Academy of Sciences, 1377,* 22–31.

Gross, M. U. M. (2006). Exceptionally gifted children: Long-term outcomes of academic acceleration and nonacceleration. *Journal for the Education of Gifted, 29,* 404–429.

Halsted, J. W. (2009). *Some of my best friends are books: Guiding gifted readers from preschool to high school* (3rd ed.). Scottsdale, AZ: Great Potential Press.

Hatt, B. (2012). Smartness as a cultural practice in schools. *American Educational Research Journal, 49,* 438–460.

Hébert, T. P., & Pagnani, A. (2010). Engaging gifted boys in new literacies. *Gifted Child Today, 33*(3), 36–45.

Hébert, T. P., & Speirs Neumeister, K. L. (2001). Guided viewing of film: A strategy for counseling gifted teenagers. *Journal of Secondary Gifted Education, 14,* 224–235.

Hertberg-Davis, H., & Callahan, C. M. (2008). A narrow escape: Gifted students' perceptions of Advanced Placement and International Baccalaureate programs. *Gifted Child Quarterly, 52,* 199–216.

Hickerson, B. (2013). Critical and creative thinking: The joy of learning! *TEMPO, 34*(2), 14–19.

Higgins, G. O. C. (1994). *Resilient adults: Overcoming a cruel past.* San Francisco, CA: Jossey-Bass.

Hornstra, L., van der Veen, I., & Peetsma, T. (2017). Effects of full-time and part-time high-ability programs on developments in students' achievement emotions. *High Ability Studies, 28,* 199–224.

Housand, A. M., Housand, B. C., & Renzulli, J. S. (2017). *Using the schoolwide enrichment model with technology.* Waco, TX: Prufrock Press.

Hussain, M., & Carignan, A. (2016). Fourth graders make inventions using SCAMPER and animal adaptation ideas. *Journal of STEM Arts, Crafts, and Constructions, 1*(2), 48–66.

International Baccalaureate Organization. (2019). *Curriculum.* Retrieved from https://www.ibo.org/programmes/diploma-programme/curriculum

Kangas, T. C., Cook, M., & Rule, A. C. (2017). Cinematherapy in gifted education identity development: Integrating the arts through STEM-themed movies. *Journal of STEM Arts, Crafts, and Constructions, 2*(2), 45–65.

Kaplan, S. N., & Gould, B. (1998). *Frames: Differentiating the core curriculum.* Las Vegas, NV: Taylor Education.

Karnes, F., & Riley, T. (1997). Developing writing through competitions. *Gifted Child Today, 20*(2), 18–19.

Kettler, T., Lamb, K. N., & Mullet, D. R. (2018). *Developing creativity in the classroom: Learning and innovation for 21st-century schools.* Waco, TX: Prufrock Press.

Kettler, T., & Margot, K. C. (2015). Aligning assessment, identification, and gifted education program services. *TEMPO, 36*(2), 13–19.

Kneebone, E. (2014). The growth and spread of concentrated poverty, 2000 to 2008-2012. *The Brookings Institution*. Retrieved from https://www.brookings.edu/interactives/the-growth-and-spread-of-concentrated-poverty-2000-to-2008-2012

Larmer, J. (2015). Gold standard PBL: Essential project design elements. *PBLWorks*. Retrieved from https://www.pblworks.org/blog/gold-standard-pbl-essential-project-design-elements

Leu, D. J., Forzani, E., Rhoads, C., Maykel, C., Kennedy, C., & Timbrell, N. (2015). The new literacies of online research and comprehension: Rethinking the reading achievement gap. *Reading Research Quarterly, 50,* 37–59.

Loveless, T. (2016). Part II: Tracking and advanced placement. *The Brookings Institution*. Retrieved from https://www.brookings.edu/research/tracking-and-advanced-placement

Malcolm, K. T., Jensen-Campbell, L. A., Rex-Lear, M., & Waldrip, A. M. (2006). Divided we fall: Children's friendships and peer victimization. *Journal of Social and Personal Relationships, 23,* 721–740.

Martin, L. T., Burns, R. M., & Schonlau, M. (2010). Mental disorders among gifted and nongifted youth: A selected review of the epidemiologic literature. *Gifted Child Quarterly, 54,* 31–41.

Matthews, G., Lin, J., Zeidner, M., & Roberts, R. D. (2017). Emotional intelligence and giftedness. In S. I. Pfeiffer (Ed.), *APA handbook of giftedness and talent* (pp. 163–182). Washington, DC: American Psychological Association.

Mayer, J. D., Caruso, D. R., & Salovey, P. (2016). The ability model of emotional intelligence: Principles and updates. *Emotion Review, 8,* 290–300.

McBee, M. T. (2006). A descriptive analysis of referral sources for gifted identification screening by race and socioeconomic status. *Journal of Advanced Academics, 17,* 103–111.

Moon, T. R., & Callahan, C. M. (2000). Performance assessment and its role in instruction of able learners. *TEMPO, 20*(4), 6–7, 19–21.

Naglieri, J. (2018). *Naglieri nonverbal ability test* (3rd ed.). Bloomington, MN: Pearson.

National Association for Gifted Children. (n.d.). *Tests and assessments.* Retrieved from https://www.nagc.org/resources-publications/gifted-education-practices/identification/tests-assessments

National Association for Gifted Children. (2009). *Nurturing social and emotional development of gifted children* [Position statement]. Retrieved from https://www.nagc.org/sites/default/files/Position%20Statement/Affective%20Needs%20Position%20Statement.pdf

National Association for Gifted Children. (2010). *NAGC Pre-K–Grade 12 Gifted Programming Standards: A blueprint for quality gifted education programs.* Washington, DC: Author.

National Association for Gifted Children. (2014). *Differentiating curriculum and instruction for gifted and talented students* [Position statement]. Retrieved from https://www.nagc.org/sites/default/files/Position%20Statement/Differentiating%20Curriculum%20and%20Instruction.pdf

National Association for Gifted Children. (2018). *Key considerations in identifying and supporting gifted and talented learners: A report from the 2018 NAGC definition task force.* Retrieved from https://www.nagc.org/sites/default/files/Position%20Statement/NAGC%20Gifted%20Definition%20Task%20Force%20Report%20%283-2019%29%282%29.pdf

Neihart, M. (2007). The socioaffective impact of acceleration and ability grouping: Recommendations for best practice. *Gifted Child Quarterly, 5,* 330–341.

Neihart, M. (2008). Identifying and providing services to twice exceptional children. In S. I. Pfeiffer (Ed.), *Handbook of giftedness in children: Psychoeducational theory, research, and best practices* (pp. 115–137). New York, NY: Springer.

Newton, A. (1995). Silver screens and silver linings: Using theater to explore feelings and issues. *Gifted Child Today, 18*(2), 14–19, 43.

Office of Superintendent of Public Instruction. (n.d.). *HiCapPLUS professional learning modules for educators.* Retrieved from https://www.k12.wa.us/student-success/learning-alternatives/highly-capable-program/hicapplus-professional-learning-modules-educators

Ogurlu, U., Yalin, H. S., & Yavuz Birben, F. (2018). The relationship between psychological symptoms, creativity, and loneliness in gifted children. *Journal for the Education of the Gifted, 41,* 193–210.

Olenchak, F. R. (2009). Effects of talents unlimited counseling on gifted/learning disabled students. *Gifted Education International, 25,* 144–164.

Olszewski-Kubilius, P., & Clarenbach, J. (2012). *Unlocking emergent talent: Supporting high achievement of low-income, high-ability students.* Washington, DC: National Association for Gifted Children.

Olszewski-Kubilius, P., & Corwith, S. (2018). Poverty, academic achievement, and giftedness: A literature review. *Gifted Child Quarterly, 62,* 37–55.

Olszewski-Kubilius, P., & Lee, S. Y. (2004). The role of participation in in-school and outside-of-school activities in the talent development of gifted students. *Journal of Secondary Gifted Education, 15*(3), 107–123.

Olszewski-Kubilius, P., & Steenbergen-Hu, S. (2017). Blending research-based practices and practice-embedded research: Project Excite closes achievement and excellence gaps for underrepresented gifted minority students. *Gifted Child Quarterly, 61,* 202–209.

Osborn, A. F. (1963). *Applied imagination: Principles and procedures of creative problem-solving* (3rd ed.). New York, NY: Scribner.

Ozturk, M. A., & Debelak, C. (2008). Affective benefits from academic competitions for middle school gifted students. *Gifted Child Today, 31,* 48–53.

Paul, R., & Elder, L. (2006). The miniature guide to critical thinking concepts and tools. *The Foundation for Critical Thinking.* Retrieved from https://www.criticalthinking.org/files/Concepts_Tools.pdf

Peters, S. J., & Engerrand, K. G. (2016). Equity and excellence: Proactive efforts in the identification of underrepresented students for gifted and talented services. *Gifted Child Quarterly, 60,* 159–171.

Peterson, J. S. (2009). Focusing on where they are: A clinical perspective. In J. L. VanTassel-Baska, T. L. Cross, & F. R. Olenchak (Eds.), *Social-emotional curriculum with gifted and talented students* (pp. 193–226). Waco, TX: Prufrock Press.

Peterson, J. S. (2012). The asset–burden paradox of giftedness: A 15-year phenomenological, longitudinal case study. *Roeper Review, 34, 1*–17.

Peterson, J. S., Betts, G., & Bradley, T. (2009). Discussion groups as a component of affective curriculum for gifted students. In J. L. VanTassel-Baska, T. L. Cross, & F. R. Olenchak (Eds.), *Social-emotional curriculum with gifted and talented students* (pp. 289–320). Waco, TX: Prufrock Press.

Plucker, J. A., & Peters, S. J. (2018). Closing poverty-based excellence gaps: Conceptual, measurement, and educational issues. *Gifted Child Quarterly, 62,* 56–67.

Powers, E. A. (2008). The use of independent study as a viable differentiation technique for gifted learners in the regular classroom. *Gifted Child Today, 31*(3), 57–65.

Rambo, K. E., & McCoach, D. B. (2012). Teacher attitudes toward subject-specific acceleration: Instrument development and validation. *Journal for the Education of the Gifted, 35,* 129–152.

Reis, S. M., Baum, S. M., & Burke, E. (2014) An operational definition of twice-exceptional learners: Implications and applications. *Gifted Child Quarterly, 58,* 217–230.

Reis, S. M., & Renzulli, J. S. (1995). *Curriculum compacting: A systematic procedure for modifying the curriculum for above average ability students.* Retrieved from https://gifted.uconn.edu/schoolwide-enrichment-model/curriculum_compacting

Reis, S. M., Westberg, K. L., Kulikowich, J. M., & Purcell, J. H. (1998). Curriculum compacting and achievement test scores: What does the research say? *Gifted Child Quarterly, 42,* 123–129.

Renzulli, J. S. (1997). *Interest-a-lyzer family of instruments.* Waco, TX: Prufrock Press.

Renzulli, J. S. (2012). Reexamining the role of gifted education and talent development for the 21st century: A four-part theoretical approach. *Gifted Child Quarterly, 56,* 150–159. doi:10.1177/00169862124 44901

Renzulli, J. S., & Reis, S. M. (2014). *The schoolwide enrichment model: A how-to guide for talent development* (3rd ed.). Waco, TX: Prufrock Press.

Renzulli, J. S., & Smith, L.H. (1979). *A guidebook for developing individualized educational programs for gifted and talented students.* Mansfield, CT: Creative Learning Press.

Rinn, A. N., & Majority, K. L. (2018). The social and emotional world of the gifted. In S. I. Pfeiffer (Ed.), *Handbook of giftedness in children: Psychoeducational theory, research, and best practices* (2nd ed., pp. 49–63). New York, NY: Springer.

Rogers, K. B. (2015). The academic, socialization, and psychological effects of acceleration: A research synthesis. In S. G. Assouline, N. Colangelo, J. VanTassel-Baska, & Lupkowski-Shoplik (Eds.), *A nation empowered: Evidence trumps the excuses holding back America's brightest students* (Vol. 2, pp. 47–57). Iowa City: University of Iowa, The Connie Belin & Jacqueline N. Blank International Center for Gifted Education and Talent Development.

Sak, U. (2004). About creativity, giftedness, and teaching creatively gifted in the classroom. *Roeper Review, 26,* 216–222.

Sawyer, R. K. (2012). *Explaining creativity: The science of human innovation* (2nd ed.). New York, NY: Oxford University Press.

Siegle, D., Gubbins, E. J., O'Rourke, P., Langley, S. D., Mun, R. U., Luria, S. R., . . . Plucker, J. A. (2016). Barriers to underserved students' participation in gifted programs and possible solutions. *Journal for the Education of the Gifted, 39,* 103–131.

Siegle, D., Wilson, H. E., & Little, C. A. (2013). A sample of gifted and talented educators' attitudes about academic acceleration. *Journal of Advanced Academics, 24,* 27–51.

Slocumb, P. D., Payne, R. K., & Williams, E. (2018). *Removing the mask: How to identify and develop giftedness in students from poverty* (3rd ed.). Highlands, TX: aha! Process.

Snyder, K. E., & Linnenbrink-Garcia, L. (2013). A developmental, person-centered approach to exploring multiple motivational pathways in gifted underachievement. *Educational Psychologist, 48,* 209–228.

Soh, K. (2017). Fostering student creativity through teacher behaviors. *Thinking Skills and Creativity, 23,* 58–66.

Speirs Neumeister, K. L., Adams, C. M., Pierce, R. L., Cassady, J. C., & Dixon, F. A. (2007). Fourth-grade teachers' perceptions of giftedness: Implications for identifying and serving diverse gifted students. *Journal for the Education of the Gifted, 30,* 479–499.

Stambaugh, T. (2014). Interview with Tamra Stambaugh on the common core and its impact on gifted education. *Davidson Institute*. Retrieved from https://www.davidsongifted.org/Search-Database/entry/A10803

Steenbergen-Hu, S., Makel, M. C., & Olszewski-Kubilius, P. (2016). What one hundred years of research says about the effects of ability grouping and acceleration on K–12 students' academic achievement: Findings of two second-order meta-analyses. *Review of Educational Research, 86,* 849–899.

Steenbergen-Hu, S., & Moon, S. M. (2011). The effects of acceleration on high-ability learners: A meta-analysis. *Gifted Child Quarterly, 55,* 39–53.

Sternberg, R. J. (2007). Who are the bright children? The cultural context of being and acting intelligent. *Educational Researcher, 36,* 148–155.

Sternberg, R. J., & Spear-Swerling, L. (2002). *Teaching for thinking*. Washington, DC: American Psychological Association.

Tan, L. S., Lee, S. S., Ponnusamy, L. D., Koh, E. R., & Tan, K .C. K. (2016). Fostering creativity in the classroom for high ability students: Context does matter. *Education Sciences, 6,* 36.

Terry, A. (2008). Student voices, global echoes: Service learning and the gifted. *Roeper Review, 30,* 45–51.

Texas Education Agency. (2009). *Texas state plan for the education of gifted/talented students*. Austin, TX: Author.

Tomlinson, C. A. (2005). Quality curriculum and instruction for highly able students. *Theory Into Practice, 44,* 160–166.

Tomlinson, C. A. (2014). *The differentiated classroom: Responding to the needs of all learners* (2nd ed.). Alexandria, VA: ASCD.

Tomlinson, C. A., & Imbeau, M. B. (2010). *Leading and managing a differentiated classroom*. Alexandria, VA: ASCD.

VanTassel-Baska, J. (2014a). Curriculum issues: Artful inquiry: The use of questions in working with gifted. *Gifted Child Today, 37,* 48–50.

VanTassel-Baska, J. (2014b). Performance-based assessment: The road to authentic learning for the gifted. *Gifted Child Today, 37,* 41–47.

VanTassel-Baska, J. (2018). Achievement unlocked: Effective curriculum interventions with low-income students. *Gifted Child Quarterly, 62,* 68–82.

VanTassel-Baska, J., & Hubbard, G. F. (2016). Classroom-based strategies for advanced learners in rural settings. *Journal of Advanced Academics, 27,* 285–310.

VanTassel-Baska, J., & Little, C. A. (Eds.). (2017). *Content-based curriculum for high-ability learners* (3rd ed.). Waco, TX: Prufrock Press.

VanTassel-Baska, J. L. (2009). Affective curriculum and instruction for gifted learners. In J. L. VanTassel-Baska, T. L. Cross, & F. R. Olenchak (Eds.), *Social-emotional curriculum with gifted and talented students* (pp. 113–132). Waco, TX: Prufrock Press.

Vogl, K., & Preckel, F. (2014). Full-time ability grouping of gifted students: Impacts on social self-concept and school-related attitudes. *Gifted Child Quarterly, 58,* 51–68.

Wechsler D. (2014). *Wechsler intelligence scale for children* (5th ed.). Bloomington, MN: Pearson.

Westberg, K. L., & Leppien, J. H. (2018). Student independent investigations for authentic learning. *Gifted Child Today, 41,* 13–18.

Williams, F. E. (1993). The cognitive-affective interaction model for enriching gifted programs. In J. S. Renzulli (Ed.), *Systems and models for developing programs for the gifted and talented* (pp. 461–484). Mansfield, CT: Creative Learning Press.

Woo, H., Bang, N. M., Cauley, B., & Choi, N. (2017). A meta-analysis: School-based intervention programs targeting psychosocial factors for gifted Racial/Ethnic minority students. *Journal for the Education of the Gifted, 40,* 199–219.

Worrell, F. C. (2009). Myth 4: A single test score or indicator tells us all we need to know about giftedness. *Gifted Child Quarterly, 53,* 242–244.

Worrell, F. C. (2014). Ethnically diverse students. In J. A. Plucker & C. M. Callahan (Eds.), *Critical issues and practices in gifted education: What the research says* (2nd ed., pp. 237–254). Waco, TX: Prufrock Press.

Worrell, F. C., & Dixson, D. D. (2018). Recruiting and retaining underrepresented gifted students. In S. I. Pfeiffer (Ed.), *Handbook of giftedness in children: Psychoeducational theory, research, and best practices* (2nd ed., pp. 209–226). New York, NY: Springer.

Zeidner, M., & Matthews, G. (2017). Emotional intelligence in gifted students. *Gifted Education International, 33,* 163–182.

Zimlich, S. L. (2017). Technology to the rescue: Appropriate curriculum for gifted students. *International Journal of Learning, Teaching and Educational Research, 16*(9), 1–12.

About the Authors

Kelly C. Margot, Ph.D., is an assistant professor at Grand Valley State University in Grand Rapids, MI. Prior to that position, she was a gifted specialist in Texas for 17 years. She received her Ph.D. in educational psychology with a concentration in gifted education from the University of North Texas. She is a gifted advocate for proper identification, appropriate curricula, ongoing research, and educating practitioners and parents.

Jacque Melin joined the faculty at Grand Valley State University in August 1999 as an affiliate faculty member. She taught classes in educational differentiation, curriculum development, and assessment practices for graduate studies in education. Jacque retired from Grand Valley in 2017 but continues to work on grants related to project-based learning and science instruction. Prior to her work at Grand Valley, Jacque was a teacher, gifted/talented coordinator, and elementary principal for Rockford Public Schools in Michigan. Jacque's degrees and certificates are from Michigan State University, Northern Michigan University, and Western Michigan University. Jacque was inducted into the Rockford Public Schools Hall of Fame for Honorary Achievement in 2012, and she received the Pew Teaching Excellence Award from Grand Valley State University in 2013. Her published books include *Passport to Learn* and *Performance Appraisal Made Easy*.

Printed in the United States
by Baker & Taylor Publisher Services